THE WIT & WISDOM OF
LITERARY
GREATS

First Edition (as *The Wit & Wisdom of Great Writers*) © 2006 House of Raven

This edition published in 2011 by Prion
An imprint of
Carlton Books Limited
20 Mortimer Street
London W1T 3JW

Typeset in Minion Pro and Frutiger 55
First edition design: David Coventon

ISBN: 978-1-85375-845-4

Printed in China

THE WIT & WISDOM OF
LITERARY GREATS

More than 800 amusing, enlightening
and downright cutting quotations

PRION

Contents

BOOKS DO FURNISH A ROOM 9 |
Books 10 | Reading 19 |

THE LITERARY ART 25 |
The Art 26 | Inspiration 31 | Style 37 |

WRITERS 47 |
On Writing 48 | On Themselves 59 |

BOOKS ARE MORE THAN BOOKS 71 |
Biography 73 | The Bible 76 | The Classics 78 |
Genre Writing 81 | Drama 89 |

POET'S CORNER 91 |
Poetry 92 | The Poets 100 |

THE CRITICAL MOMENTS 107 |
The Nature of Criticism 108 | The Critics 113 |
A critical Look/Analysis 118 |

THE SEVEN AGES OF MAN 127 |
Into The Dangerous World I Leapt 128 | Sweet Childish Days 130 |
The Hand That Rocks The Cradle 135 | School's Out 141 |
Cakes & Ale 147 | Devilish When Respectable 153 |
Rage Against The Dying Of The Light 163 |

LOVE & LUST 171 |
L'Amour 172 | The Marriage Bed 181 | When The Milk Turns Sour 187 | The 'It'
Factor 191 | Hanky Panky 195 |

TIME FOR REFLECTION 197 |
Existence 198 | Mankind 207 | Nature 215 |

MONEY MAKES THE WORLD GO ROUND 219 |
The Writer's Lot 220 | The Price Of Fame 226 |
Publish And Be Damned 230 | In Praise Of Mammon 235 |

AFFAIRS OF STATE 239 |
Government 240 | War 244 | Freedom 249 |

THE JOY OF WORDS 253 |
Language & Grammar 254 | Wordplay 265 | Wit 272 |

Index 276 |

Each quote that appears is numbered (i.e. •123). These numbers run sequentially
throughout the book. Use the index at the back to find Great writers from which
these quotes come. The index is listed in alphabetical order by surname.

To all of them.
May they live on when
txt msgng is gone

Of making many books there
is no end; and much study is
a weariness of the flesh.
Bible, Ecclesiastes 12:12 •2

He hath not fed of the
dainties that are bred
in a book; he hath not
eat paper, as it were;
he hath not drunk ink.
William Shakespeare,
Love's Labours Lost IV.ii *(1595)* •4

The English public takes
no interest in a work of art
until it is told that the work
in question is immoral.
Oscar Wilde •6

The generall end therefore
of all the booke is to fashion
a gentleman or noble person in
vertuous and gentle discipline.
Edmund Spenser, The Faerie Queene *(1596)* •3

Some books are to be tasted, others
to be swallowed, and some few to be
chewed and digested; that is, some
books are to be read only in parts;
others to be read but not curiously;
and some few to be read wholly, and
with diligence and attention. Some
books also may be read by deputy, and
extracts made of them by others.
Francis Bacon, Essays 'Of Studies' *(1625)* •5

Reformers are always finally neglected, while the memoirs of the frivolous will always be eagerly read.

Henry 'Chips' Channon,
Diary, *7 July 1936* •7

No place affords a more striking conviction of the vanity of human hopes than a public library.

Samuel Johnson, in The Rambler
23 March 1751 •8

Provided that nothing like useful knowledge could be gained from them, provided they were all story and no reflection, she had never any objection to books at all.

Jane Austen, Northanger Abbey •9

Books are good enough in their own way, but they are a mighty bloodless substitute for life.

Robert Louis Stevenson, Virginibus Puerisque
'An Apology for Idlers'
(1881) •10

The novel is not likely to die. There is no substitute, at least so far, that can handle psychological complexity and inwardness and reflection in the way that the novel can.

Julian Barnes, in Paris Review
Winter 2000-2001 •11

Every novel is a story, but life isn't one. More of a sprawl of incidents.

Doris Lessing, Under My Skin *(1994)* •12

Yes — oh dear, yes — the novel tells a story.

E.M. Forster, Aspects of the Novel *(1927)* •13

A great library contains the diary of the human race.

George Dawson, speech on opening Birmingham Free Library, 26 October 1866 •14

Yes, the collection of a lifetime and I guard it well. I never lend! Only fools lend books. All the books on this shelf once belonged to fools.

Anonymous, quoted by Bertrand Russell to C. Williams-Ellis, Architect Errant *(1971)* •15

It is a mistake to think that books have come to stay. The human race did without them for thousands of years and may decide to do without them again.
E.M. Forster, attrib. •16

All books are divisible into two classes: the books of the hour and the books of all time.
John Ruskin, Sesame and Lillies *(1865)* •17

Speak of the moderns without contempt, and of the ancients without idolatry.
Lord Chesterfield,
Letters to his Son *(1774)* •18

Art is much older than democracy, and art is uncompromisingly elitist.
Robertson Davies, lecture, Yale
20 February 1990 •19

Books will speak plain when counsellors blanch.
Francis Bacon, 'Of Counsel' *(1625)* •20

13

A book is a mirror; if an ass
peers into it, you can't expect
an apostle to look out.
Georg C Lichtenberg •21

Wealth and power are much
more likely to be the result of
breeding than they are of reading.
Fran Lebowitz, **Social Studies** *(1981)* •22

It is wonderful that even today, with
all the competition of radio, television,
films, and records, the book has kept its
precious character. A book is somehow
sacred. A dictator can kill and maim people, can sink to any kind of tyranny, and
only be hated. But when books
are burnt the ultimate tyranny has
happened. This we cannot forgive.
John Steinbeck, attrib. •23

In his library he had always been
sure of leisure and tranquillity;
and though prepared… to meet
with folly and conceit in every
other room in the house, he was
used to be free from them there.
Jane Austen, **Pride and Prejudice** *(1813)* •24

Being a librarian doesn't help. I've always found them close relatives of the walking dead.

Alan Bennett, in **Anthony Thwaite,
Larkin at Sixty** *(1982)* •25

When a man writes a letter to himself,
it is a pity to post it to somebody else.
Perhaps the same is true of a book.
D.H. Lawrence, **Aaron's Rod** *(1922)* •26

If an army of monkeys were strumming on typewriters they might write all the books in the British Museum.
Sir Arthur Eddington, English astronomer, physicist and mathematician; The Nature of the Physical World *(1928)* •27

Publishing a book is often very much like being put on trial for some offence which is quite other than the one you know in your heart you've committed.
Margaret Atwood, Negotiating with the Dead: A Writer on Writing *(2002)* •28

The multitude of books is a great evil. There is no measure or limit to this fever of writing; everyone must be an author; some out of vanity to acquire celebrity; others for the sake of lucre or gain. *Martin Luther,* Table-Talk *(1569)* •29

I'm replacing some of the timber used up by my books. Books are just trees with squiggles on them.
Hammond Innes on growing trees; interview in Radio Times *18 August 1984* •30

15

I hate books; they only teach us to talk about things we know nothing about.

Jean-Jacques Rousseau, Émile *(1762)* •31

Books do furnish a room.

Anthony Powell, title of a novel (1971) •32

Child! Do not throw this book about;
Refrain from the unholy pleasure
Of cutting all the pictures out!
Preserve it as your chiefest treasure.

Hilaire Belloc, dedication in
A Bad Child's Book of Beasts *(1896)* •33

A book is a fragile creature. It suffers the wears of time, it fears rodents, the elements, clumsy hands.

Umberto Eco •34

The Librarian was, of course, very much in favour of reading in general, but readers in particular got on his nerves…He liked people who loved and respected books, and the best way to do that, in the Librarian's opinion, was to leave them on the shelves where nature intended them to be.

Terry Pratchett, **Men at Arms** *(1993)* •35

Let your bookcases and your shelves be your gardens and your pleasure-grounds. Pluck the fruit that grows therein, gather roses, the spices and the myrrh.

Medieval Jewish philosopher Judah Ibn Tibbon, in Israel Abrahams, Jewish Life in the Middle Ages •36

Stories are like genes. They keep part of us alive after the end of our story.

A.S. Byatt, On Histories and Stories *(2000)* •39

A room without books is as a body without a soul. *Cicero* •37

When an old man dies, a library burns down.

African proverb. •38

For me, endings are never really endings. They're just there for the sake of the book.

Carol Shields, interview in Observer, *28 April 2002* •40

Take up and read, take up and read.

St. Augustine, **Confessions** •41

Reading a book is like rewriting it for yourself… You bring to… anything you read, all your experience of the world. You bring your history and you read it in your own terms.

Angela Carter, in **Marxism Today** *January 1985* •42

There are many ways of educating our feelings, but I recommend reading as that which is most ready to hand.

Robertson Davies, **lecture,** **Yale** *20 February 1990* •43

But who shall be the master? The writer or the reader?

Denis Diderot, **Jacques le Fataliste et son maître** *(1796)* •44

As soon as I put a full stop on a book, it's not my thing any more. It ceases to be mine even more when the reader picks it up.

Zadie Smith, in **Observer** *25 August 2002* •45

One writes only half the book;
the other half is with the reader.

Joseph Conrad, letter to Cunningham
Grahame, *1897* •46

What is written without
effort is in general
read without pleasure.

Samuel Johnson, in William Seward,
Biographia *(1799)* •47

The reading of good books is like
a conversation with the best men of
past centuries — in fact like a prepared
conversation, in which they reveal
only the best of their thoughts.
René Descartes, Le Discours de la
Méthode *(1637)* •48

If reading is your pleasure read, but don't
expect the magic to flow from Willa
Cather into you and the words to come
right out of your bone marrow, pre-
ordained, and arrange themselves power-
fully, perfectly, in sentences
and paragraphs. If you want to be
a writer, write. Write something.
Helen Gurley Brown, The Writer's Rules *(1998)*
•49

When I am dead,
I hope it may be said,
'His sins were scarlet,
But his books were read.'
Hilaire Belloc, 'On His Books'. *1923* •50

Choose an author as
you choose a friend.

Wentworth Dillon, Lord Roscommon,
Essay on Translated Verse *(1684)* •51

Readers and writers are united in their need for solitude… in their reach inward, via print, for a way out of loneliness.
Jonathan Franzen, **How to be Alone?** *(2002) 'Why bother?'* •52

As a reader, I want a book to kidnap me into its world. Its world must make my so-called real world seem flimsy. Its world must lure me to return. When I close the book, I should feel bereft.
Erica Jong, in **The Writer's Handbook** *(1997)* •53

A great book should leave you with many experiences, and slightly exhausted at the end. You live several lives while reading it.
William Styron, in **Writers at Work,** **first series** *(1958)* •54

If you read twenty or thirty pages by a writer, and want to continue, you are in his sea and swimming in that sea. He can write quite badly after that. Because by that time, you're in his sea, and you're moving forward.
Brian Moore, Canadian novelist, in **Rosemary Harthill, Writers Revealed** *(1989)* •55

People say that life is the thing, but I prefer reading.
Logan Pearsall Smith, **Afterthoughts** *(1931)* 'Myself' •56

Reeling and Writhing, of course, to begin with,' the Mock Turtle replied; 'and then the different branches of Arithmetic — Ambition, Distraction, Uglification, and Derision.'
Lewis Carroll, **Alice's Adventures in** **Wonderland** *(1865)* •57

The primary object of a student of literature is to be delighted. His duty is to enjoy himself: his efforts should be directed to developing his faculty of appreciation.

Lord David Cecil, **Reading as one of the Fine Arts** *(1949)* •58

Everyone probably thinks that I'm a raving nymphomaniac, that I have an insatiable sexual appetite, when the truth is I'd rather read a book.

Madonna, **Q** Magazine *1991* •59

A man ought to read just as inclination leads him; for what he reads as a task will do him little good.

Samuel Johnson, in **James Boswell, Life of Samuel Johnson** *(1791) 14 July 1763* •60

In science, read, by preference, the newest works; in literature, the oldest.

Edward George Bulwer-Lytton, **Caxtoniana** *(1863)* 'Hints on Mental Culture' •61

I think you should only read those books which bite and sting you.

Franz Kafka, **letter to Oskar Pollak,** *1904* •62

I do not hesitate to read… all good books in translations. What is really best in any book is translatable — any real insight or broad human sentiment.

Ralph Waldo Emerson, **Society and Solitude** *(1870)* •63

Reading is to the mind
what exercise is to the body.
Richard Steele, in The Tatler *18 March 1710* •64

Read not to contradict and confute,
nor to believe and take for granted,
nor to find talk and discourse,
but to weigh and consider.
Francis Bacon, Essays *(1625)* 'Of Studies' •65

There are two motives for
reading a book; one, that
you enjoy it; the other,
that you can boast about it.
Bertrand Russell, British philosopher •66

We want incident, interest, action:
to the devil with your philosophy.
Robert Louis Stevenson, letter to John
Meiklejohn, *February 1880* •67

There are times when I think
that the reading I have done
in the past has had no effect
except to cloud my mind
and make me indecisive.
*Robertson Davies, Canadian
journalist and novelist.* •68

Don't read too much now: the dude
Who lets the girl down before
The hero arrives, the chap
Who's yellow and keeps the store,
Seem far too familiar. Get stewed:
Books are a load of crap.
Philip Larkin, 'Study of Reading Habits'
(1964) •69

Magazines all too frequently
lead to books and should be
regarded by the prudent as the
heavy petting of literature.
Fran Lebowitz, Metropolitan Life, *1978* •70

Books have to be read (worse luck, it takes so long a time). It is the only way of discovering what they contain. A few savage tribes eat them, but reading is the only method of assimilation revealed to the West.
E.M. Forster •71

Four Sorts of Readers
1. Sponges that suck up everything and, when pressed give it out in the same state, only perhaps somewhat dirtier –.
2. Sand Glasses… whose reading is only a profitless measurement and dozing away of time –.
3. Straining Bags,who get rid of whatever is good and pure, and retain the dregs.
4. and lastly, the Great-Moguls' Diamond Sieves… who assuredly retain the good, while the superfluous or impure passes away and leaves no trace.
Samuel Taylor Coleridge,
Notebook, *1806-1810* •72

Reading isn't an occupation we encourage among police officers. We try to keep paper work down to a minimum. *Joe Orton,* **Loot** *(1967)* •73

The man who doesn't read good books has no advantage over the man who can't read them.
Mark Twain •74

There are worse crimes than burning books. One of them is not reading them.
Russian writer and exile
Joseph Brodsky, **remark,** *1991* •75

It's very, very easy not to be offended by a book. You just have to shut it.

Salman Rushdie, in Daily Telegraph
8 October 1994 'They Said It' •76

The last thing one knows in constructing a work is what to put first.

Blaise Pascal, Pensées *(1670)* •77

Art is meant to disturb,
science reassures.

Georges Braque, Le Jour et la nuit:
Cahiers *1917-52* •80

The acceptance that all that
is solid has melted into air,
that reality and morality are
not givens but imperfect
human constructs, is the point
from which fiction begins.

Salman Rushdie, 'Is Nothing Sacred?'
(Herbert Read Memorial Lecture)
6 February 1990 •78

Story-telling is an instinct to come
to terms with mystery, chaos, mess.

Graham Swift, in Clare Boylan (ed.) The
Agony and the Ego *(1993)* •81

Life being all inclusion
and confusion, and art
being all discrimination
and selection.

Henry James, preface to
The Spoils of Poynton *(1909 ed.)* •79

Writing is play in the same
way that playing the piano
is 'play', or putting on a
theatrical 'play' is play. Just
because something's fun
doesn't mean it isn't serious.

Margaret Atwood, in an interview,
November 1989, Earl G. Ingersoll (ed.)
(1990) •82

To invoke in oneself a feeling
one has experienced and having
evoked it in oneself then by means
of movements, lines, colours, sounds,
or forms expressed in words, so
to transmit that feeling – this is
the activity of art.

Leo Tolstoy, What is Art? *(1898)* •83

Journalism encourages haste…
and haste is the enemy of art.
Jeanette Winterson, Art Objects *(1995)* •84

True ease in writing comes
from art, not chance,

As those move easiest who
have learned to dance.
Alexander Pope, An Essay on Criticism
(1711) •85

You can't produce art by trying,
setting up exacting standards, by
talking about critical minutiae,
by the Flaubert method. It is
produced with great ease, in an
almost off-hand manner, and
without self-consciousness.
Raymond Chandler, letter to Jamie Hamilton,
17 June 1949 •86

I like to feel that a writer is perfectly
cool and detached, regarding other
people's feelings or his own, like a
God who has got beyond them.
T.S. Eliot, letter *19 September 1917* •87

I cannot imagine how it must
feel for an author to see someone
else's interpretation of their own
inner vision. I am constantly
amazed at how appreciative
most of them manage to be.
Shirley Hughes on illustration,
A Life Drawing *(2002)*•88

What we ask a theory for, is to give us back an old subject illuminated by a new light in order to realize that only from that point of view the object can be really understood.

Umberto Eco, in **Drama Review** *March 1977* •89

A writer wastes nothing.
F. Scott Fitzgerald, in Sheilah Graham and Gerald Frank, **Beloved Infidel** *(1959)* •90

One sentence. Two at most. If you can't tell yourself what your story is in one or two sentences, you're already running into trouble. Even in Moby Dick, it comes down to Captain Ahab chases a whale and doesn't get it.

Gerald Petievich, in **The Writer's Digest Handbook of Novel Writing** *(1992)* •91

To write well, express yourself like the common people, but think like a wise man.
Aristotle •92

Art requires, above all things, a suppression of one's self.
Henry James, **Mr Walt Whitman** *(1865)* •93

Anyone could write a novel given six weeks, pen, paper and no telephone or wife.
Evelyn Waugh •94

The act of writing is a kind of guerilla warfare; there is no vacation, no leave, no relief. In actuality there is very little chance of victory. You are, you fear… likely to be defeated by your own fondest dreams.
Walter Mosley, in Writers on Writing: Collected Essays from the New York Times *(2001)* •95

I believe that all those painters and writers who leave their wives have an idea at the back of their minds that their painting or writing will be the better for it, whereas they only go from bad to worse.
Patrick White, letter to Barry Humphries, *7 October 1973* •96

The true genius is a mind of large general powers, accidently determined to some particular direction.
Samuel Johnson, Lives of the English Poets *(1779-81)* •97

The only time a human being is free is when he or she makes a work of art.
Friedrich von Schiller, in Edmund White The Burning Library *(1994)* •98

Drama is life with the dull bits left out.
Alfred Hitchcock, attrib. •99

Books choose their authors; the act of creation is not entirely a rational and conscious one.
Salman Rushdie, in The Independent *4 February 1990* •100

Even the slightest thing
contains a little that is
unknown. We must find it.
To describe a blazing fire
or a tree in a plain, we must
remain before that fire or
tree until they no longer
resemble for us any other
tree or any other fire.
That is the way to
become original.

Gustave Flaubert advising
Guy de Maupassant; recalled
by de Maupassant in Preface,
Pierre et Jean *(1888)* •101

Nothing has yet been said that's not been said before.

Terence, Eunuchu •102

For a start, I've got to be out of my head to write.
Shane MacGowan of The Pogues (1989) •103

To turn events into ideas is the function of literature.
George Santayana, attrib. •104

It came from mine own heart.
   So to my head

And thence into my fingers
   it tricklèd;

Then to my pen, from whence
   immediately

On paper I did dribble
   it daintily.

John Bunyan, The Holy War '
Advice to the Reader'*(1682)* •105

But words come halting forth, wanting
   Invention's stay;

Invention, Nature's child, fled step-dame
   Study's blows…

Biting my truant pen, beating myself
   for spite,

'Fool,' said my Muse to me; 'look in
   thy heart and write.'

Philip Sidney, Astrophil and Stella,
Sonnet 1 *(1591)* •106

All writers know that on some golden
mornings they are touched by the wand
— are on intimate terms with poetry
and cosmic truth. I have
experienced these moments myself.
Their lesson is simple: It's a total illusion.
And the danger in the illusion is that
you will wait for those moments.
J.K. Galbraith •107

The process of writing… consists of sitting in one place for several hours every day and groaning immoderately while you make marks of one colour on a surface of another. Inspiration has precious little to do with it and brutal toil a great deal.

Richard Ford, in Writer's on Writing: Collecting Essays from The New York Times *(2001)*•108

I don't know anything about inspiration because I don't know what inspiration is — I've heard about it, but I never saw it.
William Faulkner, interview in Paris Review, *Spring 1956* •109

The childhoods of writers are thought to have something to do with their vocation, but when you look at these childhoods they are in fact very different. What they often contain, however, are books and solitude.
Margaret Atwood, Negotiating with the Dead: A Writer on Writing *(2002)* •110

Write while the heat is in you… The writer who postpones the recording of his thoughts uses an iron which has cooled to burn a hole with. He cannot inflame the minds of his audience.
Henry David Thoreau, letter, *1 February 1852* •111

If you are in difficulties with a book, try the element of surprise: attack it at an hour when it isn't expecting it.
H.G. Wells •112

The pen is the tongue of the mind.

Miguel de Cervantes •113

What do you think of the world? You, the prism, measure the light of the world; it burns through your mind to throw a different spectroscopic reading onto white paper than anyone else anywhere can throw.

Ray Bradbury, Zen in the Art of Writing *(1990)*•114

Unfortunately for novelists, real life is getting way too funny and far-fetched. It's especially true in Miami, where the daily news seems to be scripted by David Lynch. Fact is routinely more fantastic than fiction.

Carl Hiaasen, in Writers on Writing: Collected Essays from the New York Times •115

He has gained every point who has mixed profit with pleasure, by delighting the reader at the same time as instructing him.

Horace, Ars Poetica •116

Think before you speak is criticism's motto; speak before you think creation's.

E.M. Forster, Two Cheers for Democracy *(1951)* •117

33

The more indignant I make the bourgeois, the happier I am.

Gustave Flaubert, **letter,** *25 July 1842* •118

There is a splinter of ice in the heart of a writer.

Graham Greene, explaining why he was fascinated by witnessing the death of a child while he was in hospital recovering from appendicitis; in **A Sort of Life** *(1971)* •119

When starting to think about any novel, part of the motive is: I'm going to show them, this time. Without that, a lot of what passes under the name of creative energy would be lost.

Kingsley Amis, in **George Greenfield, Scribblers for Bread** *(1989)* •120

Each year brings new problems of Form and Content, new foes to tug with: at Twenty I tried to vex my elders, past Sixty it's the young whom I hope to bother.

W.H. Auden, **Shorts I** •121

Asked why he wrote The Name of the Rose: "I felt like poisoning a monk." *Umberto Eco, in* **George Plimpton (ed.) The Writer's Chapbook** *(1989)* •122

I draw from life —
but I always pulp my
acquaintance before
serving them up. You
would never recognize
a pig in a sausage.

Frances 'Fanny' Trollope, English novelist,
in S. Baring-Gould, Early Reminiscences
1834-1864 *(1923). Remark made c.1848* •123

Why does my Muse only speak
  when she is unhappy?

She does not, I only listen when I
  am unhappy

When I am happy I live and
  despise writing

For my Muse this cannot but
  be dispiriting.
    Stevie Smith, My Muse *(1964)* •124

It's easier to write about
things that are falling
apart than things that
are beautiful and perfect.
Beck, American Singer/Songwriter (1996)•125

Tragedy is thus a representation
of an action that is worth serious
attention, complete in itself and
of some amplitude… by means
of pity and fear bringing about
the purgation of such emotions.
Aristotle, Poetics •126

The composition of a tragedy
requires testicles.

Voltaire, on being asked why no woman
had ever written 'a tolerable tragedy'; **letter**
to Byron from John Murray, *2 April 1817* •127

In every first novel the
hero is the author as
Christ or as Faust.

Oscar Wilde, **attrib.** •128

The original writer is not he who
refrains from imitating others, but
he who can be imitated by none.

François-René Chateaubriand,
Le Génie du Christianisme *(1802)* •130

Show me a hero
and I will write
you a tragedy.

F. Scott Fitzgerald, **The Crack-Up** *(1936)* •129

Unless the almighty maker
them ordain

His dark materials to create
more worlds

John Milton, **Paradise Lost** *(1667)* •131

One of the disabling weaknesses of current Western literature is its unwillingness or inability to engage with the dance of the spirit in the sciences. Music and the arts are equipped to do better.

George Steiner, 'A Festival Overture' (Edinburgh University Festival Lecture, *August 1996* •132

No story comes from nowhere; new stories are born from old — it is the new combinations that make them new.

Salman Rushdie, Haroun and the Sea of Stories *(1990)* •133

The web, then, or the pattern; a
web at once sensuous and logical,
an elegant and pregnant texture:
that is style, that is the foundation
of the art of literature.
Robert Louis Stevenson, The Art of Writing
(1905) 'On some technical Elements of Style
in Literature' *(written 1885)* •134

I know of only one rule: style
cannot be too clear, too simple.
Stendhal, letter to Balzac, *30 October 1840* •135

An author arrives at a good
style when his language performs
what is required of it without
shyness. *Cyril Connolly,* Enemies of
Promise *(1938)* •136

Proper words in proper places,
make the true definition of a style.
Jonathan Swift, Letter to a Young
Gentleman lately entered into Holy Orders
9 January 1720 •137

Prose is architecture,
not interior decoration,
and the Baroque
is over. *Ernest Hemingway, in*
Jeffrey Meyers, Hemingway
(1985) •138

Good prose is like a window-pane.
George Orwell, **Collected Essays vol.1**
'Why I Write' *(1968)* •139

Every author of some value transgresses against 'good style', and in that transgression lies the originality (and hence the raison d'être) of his art.
Milan Kundera, **Testaments Betrayed** *(1995)* •140

The only obligation
to which in advance
we may hold a novel,
without incurring the
accusation of being
arbitrary, is that
it be interesting.
Henry James,
The Art of Fiction *(1888)* •141

To find a form that
accommodates the mess,
that is the task
of the artist now.
An ever optimistic Samuel Beckett,
Proust *(1961)* •142

A writer must be as objective as a chemist: he must abandon the subjective; he must know that a dung-heap plays a very reasonable part in landscape, and that evil passions are as inherent in life as good ones. *Anton Chekhov,*
letter to M.V. Kiselev,
14 January 1887 •143

There is no such thing as a moral or immoral book. Books are well written, or badly written.
Oscar Wilde, **The Picture of Dorian Gray** *(1891)* •144

What a book a devil's chaplain might write on the clumsy, wasteful, blundering, low, and horridly cruel works of nature!

Charles Darwin, letter to J.D. Hooker, *13 July 1856* •145

Oh! It is only a novel!... only Cecilia, or Camilla, or Belinda: or, in short, only some work in which the most thorough knowledge of human nature, the happiest delineation of its varieties, the liveliest effusions of wit and humour are conveyed to the world in the best chosen language.

Jane Austen, Northanger Abbey *(1818)* •146

Style and structure are the essence of a book; great ideas are hogwash.

Vladimir Nabokov, in George Plimpton (ed.), Writers at Work *(4th series, 1977)* •147

The structure of a play is always the story of how the birds came home to roost.

Arthur Miller, in Harper's Magazine *August 1958* •148

The famous rules, which the French call Des Trois Unitéz, or the Three Unities, which ought to be observed in every regular play; namely, of Time, Place, and Action.

John Dryden, A Essay of Dramatic Poesy *(1668)* •149

Grasp the subject,
the words will follow.
Cato the Elder •150

There is nothing to write about,
you say. Well then, write and let
me know just this — that there is
nothing to write about; or tell me
in the good old style if you are well.
Pliny the Younger, Letters •151

The writer's problem is, how
to strike the balance between
the uncommon and the ordinary
so as on the one hand to give
interest, and on the other to
give reality. *Thomas Hardy,*
notebook *July 1881* •152

The province of literature is a
debatable line. It lies on the confines
of two distinct territories. It is under
the jurisdiction of two hostile powers;
and like other districts similarly situated
it is ill-defined, ill-cultivated, and ill-
regulated. Instead of being equally
shared between its two rulers, the
Reason and the Imagination, it falls
alternately under the sole and absolute
dominion of each. It is sometimes fiction.
It is sometimes theory.
Lord Macaulay, History *(1828)* •153

Having to read footnotes
resembles having to go
downstairs to answer the
door while in the midst
of making love.
Noël Coward •154

It is sometimes necessary
to repeat what we all know.
All mapmakers should place
the Mississippi in the same
location, and avoid originality.

Saul Bellow, **Mr Sammler's Planet** *(1970)* •155

In nearly all good fiction, the basic
— all but inescapable — plot form is:
a central character wants something,
goes after it despite opposition
(perhaps including his own doubts),
and so arrives at a win, lose, or draw.

John Gardner, **On Becoming a Novelist** *(1983)*
•156

'Where shall I begin, please your
Majesty?' he asked. 'Begin at the
beginning,' the King said gravely,
'and go on till you come to the
end: then stop.'

Lewis Carroll, **Alice's Adventures
in Wonderland** *(1865)* •157

My way is to begin
with the beginning.

Lord Byron, **Don Juan** *(1819-24)* •158

'The king died and then the queen died',
is a story. 'The king died and then the
queen died of grief' is a plot.

E.M. Forster, **Aspects of the Novel** *(1927)* •159

Sir, Perhaps the lack of literary
inventiveness in modern opening
lines is due to the effect of the
word processor. When I ran
the first line of Moby Dick
through my spell-checker, it
suggested changing this to
'Call me Fishmeal'.

Helen Grayson, **letter to
The Times** *18 October 1997* •160

When I sit down to write a novel
I do not at all know, and I do not
very much care, how it is to end.
Anthony Trollope, **Autobiography** *(1883)* •161

The beginning of a book holds more
apprehensions for the novelist than
the ending. After living with a book
for a year or two, he has to come
to terms with his unconsciousness
— the end will be imposed. But if
a book is started in the wrong way,
it may never be finished.
Graham Greene, **In Search of a Character**
(1961) •162

It has always seemed to me
as unnatural for two people
to write a book together as
for three people to have a
baby. *Evelyn Waugh is suspicious of*
literary collaboration, **letter,**
30 July 1962 •163

Great things of course have
been done by solitary workers;
but they have usually been
done with double the pains
they would have if they had
been produced in more genial
circumstances.
Henry James, **Hawthorne** *(1879)* •164

A sequel is an
admission that you've
been reduced to
imitating yourself.
Don Marquis, US writer •165

With each book you write you should lose the admirers you gained with the previous one.

André Gide, in **Edmund White, The Burning Library** *(1994)* •166

I am of the opinion that the reader each writer wants is part and parcel of the novel's conception. His special presence is evoked in the style and texture of each line. What we call style is the explicit inclusion of some readers in, and all other readers out.

Wright Morris, in **Afterwords: Novelists on Their Novels** *(1969)* •167

When you're a novelist, you're writing a play but you're acting all the parts, you're controlling the lights and the scenery and the whole business, and it's your show.

Robertson Davies, in **Paris Review** *1989* •168

Journalism is about working yourself up into a lather over things you previously felt nothing about. It is diametrically opposed to what you do as a novelist, which is very slowly to discover what it is you really think about things.

Kazuo Ishiguro, in **The Guardian** *15 May 1996* •169

The chief difference between good writing and better writing may be measured by the number of imperceptible hesitations the reader experiences as he goes along. The author functions as a kind of forest guide. Does our reader trip over unfamiliar words…stub his toe on an ambiguous antecedent?

James J. Kilpatrick, **The Writer's Art** *(1984)* •170

A good novel tells us the truth about its hero; but a bad novel tells us the truth about its author.

G.K. Chesterton, **Heretics** *(1905)* •171

The most important advice I would suggest to beginning writers: try to leave out the parts that readers skip.

Elmore Leonard, in **Snoopy's Guide to the Writing Life** *(2002)* •172

There is a magical quality in names. To change the name is to change the character.

Graham Greene, **Ways of Escape** *(1980)*•173

My theory of writing I can sum up in one sentence. An author ought to write for youth in his own generation, the critics of the next, and the schoolmasters of ever after.

F. Scott Fitzgerald, **letter to the Booksellers' Convention,** *April 1920* •174

Only two classes of books are of universal appeal. The very best and the very worst. *Ford Madox Ford,* **Joseph Conrad** *(1924)* •175

What the American public always wants is a tragedy with a happy ending.

William Dean Howells explains to Edith Wharton why her play The House of Mirth *wouldn't run on Broadway.*
October 1906, in R.W.B. Lewis, Edith Wharton *(1975)* •176

But those who cannot write,
  and those who can,

All rhyme, and scrawl, and scribble,
  to a man.

Alexander Pope, Imitations of Horace
(1737) •177

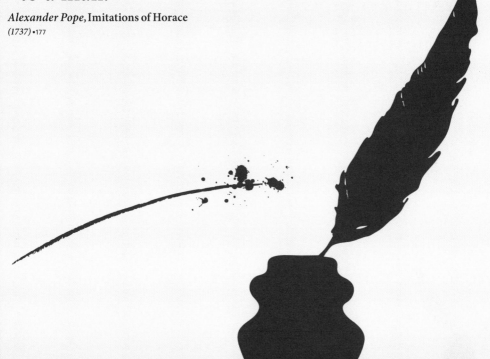

So all my best is dressing
  old words new,

Spending again what is
  already spent.

William Shakespeare, Sonnet 76 •178

Writing, Madam, is a mechanic part of wit; a gentleman should never go beyond a song or a billet.

Sir George Etheridge,
English Restoration dramatist;
The Man of Mode *(1676)* •179

The only end of writing is to
enable the readers better to
enjoy life, or better to endure it.

Samuel Johnson, A Free Enquiry *(1757)* •180

Read over your compositions,
and where ever you meet with
a passage which you think is
particularly fine, strike it out.

Samuel Johnson, quoting a college tutor,
James Boswell, Life of Samuel Johnson *(1791)*
30 April 1773 •181

Three or four families in a country village is the very thing to work on.

Jane Austen, letter to Anna Austen,
9 September 1814 •182

A person who can write a long letter, with ease, cannot write ill. *Jane Austen, Miss Bingley in* **Pride & Prejudice** •183

People don't deserve to have good writing, they are so pleased with bad. *Ralph Waldo Emerson,* **Journals** *1841* •185

Remove at least fifty superlatives in each chapter. Never say 'Oliver's burning passion for Helen.' The poor novelist has to make us believe in the burning passion without ever naming it: that would be immodest. *Stendhal,* letter to Mme Gaulthier, *4 May 1834* •18

The hero of my tale — whom I love with all the power of my soul, whom I have tried to portray in all his beauty, who has been, and is, and will be beautiful — is Truth. *Leo Tolstoy,* **Sebastopol in May** *(1855)* •186

Since when was genius found respectable?

Elizabeth Barrett Browning, **Aurora Leigh** *(1857)* •187

But a man or woman who publishes writings inevitably assumes the office of teacher or influences the public mind... He can no more escape the moral taste, and with it the action of the intelligence, than a setter of fashion in furniture and dress can fill the shops with his designs and leave the garniture of persons and houses unaffected by his industry.
George Eliot, attrib. •188

No man would have dared to write and publish such books... no man could have written such delineations of female passion... No! They are women, who by their writings have been doing the work of the enemy of souls... Women... who might have been bright and shining lights in their generation. *Francis E. Paget,* Lucretia *(1868)* •189

Genius does what it must, and Talent does what it can.
Owen Meredith, Last Words of a Sensitive Second-Rate Poet *(1868)* •190

Persons attempting to find a motive in this narrative will be prosecuted; persons attempting to find a moral in it will be banished; persons attempting to find a plot in it will be shot.
Mark Twain, The Adventures of Huckleberry Finn *(1884)* •191

If there is anything said in two sentences that could have been as clearly and as engagingly said in one, then it's amateur work.
Robert Louis Stevenson, letter to William Archer, *February 1888* •192

One should never make one's debut with a scandal. One should reserve that to give an interest to one's old age.
Oscar Wilde, The Picture of Dorian Gray, *(1891)* •193

As to the Adjective:
when in doubt, strike
it out. *Mark Twain,*
Pudd'nhead Wilson *(1894)* •194

Enduring fame is promised
only to those writers who can
offer to successive generations
a substance constantly renewed;
for every generation arrives
upon the scene with its own
particular hunger. *André Gide,*
Pretexts *(1903)* •195

Omit needless words… A sentence
should contain no unnecessary words,
a paragraph no unnecessary sentences,
for the same reason that a drawing
should have no unnecessary lines
and a machine no unnecessary parts.
William Strunk, **The Elements of Style** *(1918)*
•196

It is wonderful how much news
there is when people write every
other day; if they wait for a month,
there is nothing that seems worth
telling. *O. Douglas,* **Penny Plain** *(1920)* •197

An average English word is four letters and a half.
By hard, honest labour I've dug all the large words
out of my vocabulary and shaved them down till
the average is three and a half letters… I never
write metropolis for seven cents because I can get
the same money for city. I never write policeman,
because I can get the same money for Cop.
Mark Twain, **Mark Twain's Speeches** *(1923)*
•198

To my daughter Leonora without whose
never-failing sympathy and encouragement
this book would have been finished in
half the time. *P.G. Wodehouse, dedication,*
The Heart of a Goof *(1926)* •199

What no wife of a writer can ever understand is that a writer is working when he's staring out of the window.

Burton Rascoe, American newspaper editor.
•200

A woman must have money and a room of her own if she is to write fiction.

Virginia Woolf, A Room of One's Own *(1929)* •201

The moment a man sets his thoughts down on paper, however secretly, he is in a sense writing for publication.

Raymond Chandler, working notes on the Julia Wallace murder case, in **Raymond Chandler Speaking** *(1962)* •202

We write to taste life twice, in the moment, and in retrospection... We write to be able to transcend our life, to reach beyond it. We write to teach ourselves to speak with others, to record our journey into the labyrinth.

Anais Nin •203

Literature is mostly about having sex and not much about having children. Life is the other way round.

David Lodge, **The British Museum is Falling Down** *(1965)* •204

Beware of writing to me. I always answer… My father spent the last 20 years of his life writing letters. If someone thanked him for a present, he thanked them for thanking him and there was no end to the exchange but death.

Novelist Evelyn Waugh, son of noted editor and publisher Arthur Waugh; letter to Lady Mosley, *30 March 1966* •205

There are three reasons for becoming a writer. The first is that you need the money; the second, that you have something to say that you think the world should know; and the third is that you can't think what to do with the long winter evenings.

Quentin Crisp, The Naked Civil Servant *(1968)* •206

The idea of being a writer attracts a good many shiftless people, those who are merely burdened with poetic feelings or afflicted with sensibility.

Flannery O'Connor, in Mystery and Manners *(1969)* •207

Ridicule is the only honourable weapon we have left.

Muriel Spark, The Desegregation of Art *(1971)* •208

You shouldn't pay very much attention to anything writers say. They don't know why they do what they do. They're like good tennis players or good painters, who are just full of nonsense, pompous and embarrassing.

John Barth, in The Contemporary Writer *(1972)* •209

Each writer is born with a repertory company in his head. Shakespeare has perhaps twenty players, and Tennessee Williams has about five, and Samuel Beckett one — and maybe a clone of that one. I have ten or so, and that's a lot. As you get older, you become more skilful at casting them. *Gore Vidal, in* **Times Herald** **(Dallas)** *18 June 1978* •210

Everyone thinks that writers must know more about the inside of the human head, but that is wrong. They know less, that's why they write: trying to find out what everyone else takes for granted. *Margaret Atwood,* **Dancing Girls and Other Stories** *(1982)* •211

The writer must be universal in sympathy and an outcast by nature: only then can he see clearly. *Julian Barnes,* **Flaubert's Parrot** *(1984)* •212

If you can't annoy somebody, there's little point in writing.
Kingsley Amis •213

If you want your writing to be taken seriously, don't marry and have kids, and above all, don't die. But if you do have to die, commit suicide. They approve of that. *Ursula Le Guin,* **Prospects for Women in Writing** *(1986)* •214

54

A writer's visible life and the root of imagination do not connect above ground.

Mavis Gallant, **Paris Notebooks: Essays and Reviews** *(1986)* •215

Writers live twice. They go along with their regular life… But there's another part of them that they have been training. The one that lives everything a second time. That sits down and sees their life again and goes over it. Looks at the texture and the details. *Natalie Goldberg,* **Writing Down the Bones** *(1986)* •216

Writing is like driving at night in the fog. You can only see as far as your headlights, but you can make the whole trip that way.

US writer E.L. Doctorow, in **George Plimpton, Writers at Work** *(1988)* •217

I don't use a typewriter. It's too heavy, too much trouble. I use a notebook, and I write in my bed. Ninety-five percent of everything I've written has been done in bed.

Paul Bowles, in **George Plimpton** (ed.) **The Writer's Chapbook** *(1989)* •218

My pen… is a Waterman's, black enamel with a trim of gold. When I write with it, I feel as if I'm wearing a perfectly tailored suit, and my hair is pulled back into a chignon.

Mary Gordon, in Writers on Writing: Collected Essays from The New York Times *(2001)* •219

In the mid-eighties I was a grateful convert to computers… I like the provisional nature of unprinted material held in the computer's memory — like an unspoken thought.

Ian McEwan, in Paris Review, *2002* •220

If a writer writes truthfully out of individual experience then what is written inevitably speaks for other people. For thousands of years storytellers have taken for granted that their experiences must be general. It never occurred to them that it is possible to divorce oneself from life.

Doris Lessing, in Partisan Review, *Fall 1992* (special issue) 'Unexamined Mental Attidudes Left Behind by Communism'. •221

All writers are thieves; theft is a necessary tool of the trade.

Nina Bawden, Mothers: Reflections by Daughters *(1995)* •222

Most novelists, knowing that ongoing work is fed by ongoing life, prize their telephones, their correspondence, and their daily rubbing up against family and friends.
Carol Shields, Jane Austen *(2001)* •223

Writers, those professionals of dissatisfaction.

Susan Sontag, in Writers on Writing: Collected Essays from the New York Times *(2001)* •224

I love deadlines. I love the whooshing noise they make as they go by.
Douglas Adams; in The Guardian *14 May 2001* •225

The boundaries of science have expanded in recent decades in a rather interesting way. Emotion, consciousness, human nature itself, have become legitimate topics for the biological sciences. And these subjects of course are of central interest to the novelist. The invasion of our territory ought to be fruitful. *Ian McEwan, in* Paris Review, *2002* •226

If I had to give young writers advice, I would say don't listen to writers talk about writing or themselves.

Lillian Hellman, American playwright. •227

That is one last thing to remember: Writers are always selling somebody out.

Joan Didion, Slouching Toward Bethlehem, preface *(1968)* •228

When I was a little boy,
they called me a liar, but
now that I am grown up,
they call me a writer.

Polish-born American writer Isaac Bashevis Singer, in Bibliophile *July 1986* •229

Whoa, there's enough,
whoa now, little book!
We have got to the post!
But you want to go on further
and keep going, there's no
holding you at the final sheet,
as though you had not finished
the business which was
finished even on page one.

Martial, Epigrammata •230

It could be said that in this book I have only made up a bunch of other men's flowers, providing of my own only the string that ties them together.

Montaigne, Essais *(1580)* •231

I write of melancholy,
by being busy to
avoid melancholy.

Robert Burton, The Anatomy of Melancholy *(1621-51)* 'Democritus to the Reader' •232

I desire to set before my
fellows the likeness of a man
in all the truth of nature,
and that man myself.
Jean-Jacques Rousseau,
Confessions *(1782)* •233

I think I may boast myself to be,
with all possible vanity, the most
unlearned and uninformed female
who ever dared to be an authoress.
Jane Austen, **letter** *11 December 1815* •234

No, indeed, I am never
too busy to think of S.
And S. I can no more
forget it than a mother can
forget her suckling child.
Jane Austen, **letter to her sister, Cassandra**
•235

I am going to take a heroine whom
no-one but myself will much like.
Jane Austen, on starting **Emma,** *in* **J.E.
Austen-Leigh, A Memoir of Jane Austen**
(1926 ed.) •236

Between you and me,
I am not deep, but I
am very wide, and it
takes time to walk
around me.
Honoré de Balzac, **letter to
Countess Maffei,** *1837* •237

To such critics
I would say; 'to you
I am neither man
nor woman —
I come before you
as an author only.'

Charlotte Brontë, **letter to**
W.S. Williams, *16 August 1849* •238

When I want to read
a novel, I write one.

Benjamin Disreali, in **W. Monypenny and**
G. Buckle, Life of Benjamin Disreali vol.6
(1920) •239

It is splendid to be a great writer,
to put men into the frying pan
of your words and make them
pop like chestnuts. *Gustave Flaubert,*
letter *3 November 1851*
•240

I cannot write books
handling the topics of
the day; it is of no use
trying. Nor can I write
a book for its moral.

Charlotte Brontë, **letter to George Smith,**
30 October 1852 •241

An author who talks about his own
books is almost as bad as a mother
who talks about her own children.
Benjamin Disraeli •242

I have many irons in the fire, and am bursting with writableness.

Henry James, letter *29 May 1878* •243

I wrote such melancholy things when I was young that I am obliged to be unusually cheerful and robust in my old age.

Christina Rossetti, in Jan Marsh, Christina Rossetti *(1994)* •244

Medicine is my lawful wife and literature is my mistress. When I get tired of one I spend the night with the other. *Anton Chekhov,* letter to A.S. Suvorin, *11 September 1888* •245

When I face that fatal manuscript it seems to me that I have forgotten how to think — worse! how to write. It is as if something in my head had given way to let in a cold grey mist. I knock about in it till I am positively, physically sick. *Joseph Conrad,* letter, *5 August 1896* •246

I never accepted a knighthood because to be me is honour enough.

George Bernard Shaw •247

I can live for two months on a good compliment.
Mark Twain •248

The port from which I set out was, I think, that of the essential loneliness of my life.
Henry James, letter, *2 October 1900* •249

After all, one knows one's weak points so well, that it's rather bewildering to have the critics overlook them and invent others.
Edith Wharton, letter, *19 November 1909* •251

After my marriage, she edited everything I wrote. And what is more — she not only edited my works — she edited me! *Mark Twain of his wife, Livy; in* Van Wyck Brooks, The Ordeal of Mark Twain *(1920)* •250

I hate the sort of licence that English people give themselves… to spread over and flop and roll about. I feel as fastidious as though I wrote with acid.
Katherine Mansfield, letter to John Middleton Murry, *19 May 1913* •252

The business of selection and revision is simply hell for me — my efforts to cut out 50,000 words may sometimes result in my adding 75,000.

American novelist Thomas Wolfe, **letter to Maxwell Perkins, his editor at Scribner's,** *17 November 1928* •253

My memory is certainly in my hands. I can remember things only if I have a pencil and I can write with it and play with it. I think your hand concentrates for you. *Rebecca West, in* George Plimpton **(ed.) The Writer's Chapbook** *(1989)* •254

It scarcely needs criticism to bring home to me that much of my work has been slovenly, haggard and irritated, most of it hurriedly and inadequately revised, and some of it as white and pasty in its texture as a starch-fed nun.

H.G. Wells, **Experiment in Autobiography** *(1934)* •255

I was driven into writing because I found it was the only way a lazy and ill-educated man could make a decent living. I am not complaining about the wages. They always seemed to me disproportionately high. What I mind so much is the work. *Evelyn Waugh, in* **Nash's Pall Mall Magazine,** *March 1937* •256

You know you're writing well when you're throwing good stuff into the wastebasket.

Ernest Hemingway, **attrib.** •257

I often covered more than a hundred sheets of paper with drafts, revisions, rewritings, ravings, doodlings, and intensely concentrated work to produce a single verse.

Dylan Thomas, **letter,**
25 May 1948 •258

Better to write for yourself and have no public, than write for the public and have no self.

Cyril Connolly, in **Pritchett (ed.),
Turnstile One** •259

If I had to choose between betraying my country and betraying my friend, I hope I should have the guts to betray my country. *Novelist E M Forster,*
'What I Believe', *in* **Two
Cheers for Democracy,**
1951 •260

I am a drinker with a writing problem.

Brendan Behan •261

From the time I was nine or ten, it was a toss-up whether I was going to be a writer or a painter, and I discovered by the time I was sixteen or seventeen that paints cost too much money, so I became a writer because you could be a writer with a pencil and a penny notebook.

*Irish novelist and short-story writer
Frank O'Connor, in* **George Plimpton (ed.)
The Writer's Chapbook** *(1989)* •262

I always start with a title… and then work round different meanings. A novel is, for me, always an elaboration of the title.

Muriel Spark, in Scotsman *1962* •263

The ideal reader of my novels is a lapsed Catholic and a failed musician, short-sighted, colour-blind, auditorily biased, who has read the books that I have read. He should also be about my age.

Anthony Burgess, in **George Plimpton (ed.), Writers at Work 4th Series** *(1977)* •266

A doormat in a world of boots.

A self-assessment from novelist and short-story writer Jean Rhys; quoted in Guardian *6 December 1990* •264

I am the kind of writer that people think other people are reading.

V.S. Naipaul, in Radio Times *14 March 1979* •267

The writer's abiding problem is that he gets so sick of his own company but daren't take too long away from it.

Peter Nichols, Diary, *2 January 1973* •265

I sometimes lose interest in the characters and get much more interested in the trees and animals.

Toni Morrison, in **George Plimpton (ed.) The Writer's Chapbook** *(1989)* •268

It's probably a form of childish curiosity that keeps me going as a fiction writer. I… want to open everybody's bureau drawers and see what they keep in there. I'm nosy.

Margaret Atwood, in an interview, December 1986; **in Earl G. Ingersoll (ed.) Margaret Atwood: Conversations** *(1990)* •269

I always think of my novels as being the lives of the characters.

Patrick White, **Patrick White Speaks** *(1990)* •270

Details fascinate me.
I love to pile up details.
They create an atmosphere.

Muriel Spark, **Curriculum Vitae** *(1992)* •271

I'm not too keen on characters taking over; they do as they are damn well told.

Iain Banks, in **Stan Nicholls (ed.) Wordsmiths of Wonder** *(1993)* •272

When I read something saying I've not done anything as good as Catch-22 I'm tempted to reply, 'Who has?'

Joseph Heller, in **The Times** *9 June 1993* •273

I need people's good opinion. This is something in myself I dislike because I even need the good opinion of people I don't admire. I am afraid of them. I am afraid of what they will say to me. I am afraid of their tongues and their indifference.

Ruth Rendell, in **Anthony Clare, In the Psychiatrist's Chair II** *(1995)* •274

I am as shallow as a puddle.

Helen Fielding, creator of **Bridget Jones** •275

My writing is like fine wine; the more you read, the more you get from it. Reading it once is like taking a dog to the theatre.

V.S. Naipaul, winner of the **Nobel Prize for Literature** •276

Self-knowledge does not necessarily help a novelist. It helps a human being a great deal but novelists are often appalling human beings.

Peter Carey •277

For me it's therapy. Anything that's going on in my life, anything like that, I just give to Rebus as a plot. So I'm working through my worries through him.

Ian Rankin, in **Observer** *18 March 2001* •278

I can do to him whatever I like. I'm allowed to torture him as much as I want. He's mine.
J.K. Rowling defends her right to put **Harry Potter** *through the mill* •279

It felt as if some woman had come out of nowhere saying she was my daughter's mother.
J.K. Rowling on being falsely accused of plagiarism; in The Times *20 September 2002* •280

Slowly but surely the pen became mightier than the double-quick pick-up timestep with shuffle.
Zadie Smith, on her shifting ambitions from dancer to author, in Independent *7 September 2002* •281

I write because I want more than one life; I insist on a wider selection. It's greed, plain and simple. When my characters join the circus, I'm joining the circus. Although I'm happily married, I spent a great deal of time mentally living with incompatible husbands.
Anne Tyler, Pulitzer Prize-winning American writer •282

What to do with
all this talent, how
to stay alive until
I've gotten down
to it. I still feel that.

Saul Bellow to his biographer on 30 August 1992, in New Yorker
26 June 1995 •283

A well-written life is almost as rare as a well-spent one.

Thomas Carlyle, Critical and Miscellaneous Essays *(1838)* John Paul Friedrich Richter' •284

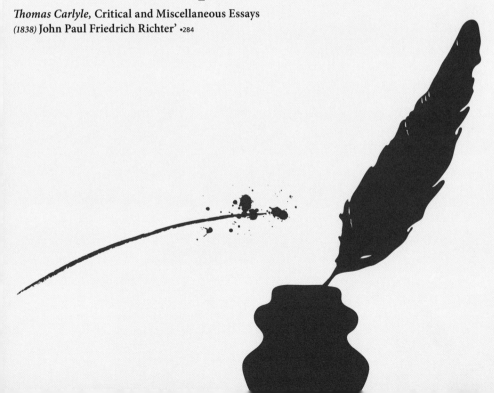

Nobody can write the life
of a man, but those who have
eat and drunk and lived in
social intercourse with him.
Samuel Johnson, in James Boswell, Life
of Samuel Johnson *(1791) 31 March 1772* •285

Biographers know nothing about
the intimate sex lives of their own wives,
but they think they know
all about Stendhal's or Faulkner's.
Milan Kundera, Testaments Betrayed *(1995)*
•287

Biographies are likely either to be acts of worship or acts of destruction. And the best ones have elements of both.

*Biographer and childrens author Humphrey
Carpenter, in conversation with Lyndall
Gordon; in* John Batchelor (ed.), The Art of
Literary Biography *(1995)* •286

I read biographies backwards,
beginning with the death.
If that takes my fancy I go
through the rest. Childhood
seldom interests me at all.
Alan Bennett, Writing Home *(1994)* •288

Formerly we used to canonise our
heroes. The modern method is to
vulgarise them. Cheap editions of
great books may be delightful,
but cheap editions of great men
are absolutely detestable.
Oscar Wilde, The True Function
and Value of Criticism, *1890.* •289

Biography is in some ways the most brutish of all the arts. It shifts about uncomfortably in the strangely uncertain middle ground between deliberate assassination and helpless boot-licking.

Dennis Potter, in The Times
24 February 1968 •290

Every great man nowadays has his disciples, and it is always Judas who writes the biography.

Oscar Wilde, Intentions *(1891)*
The Critic as Artist •291

Anyone turning biographer commits himself to lies, to concealment, to hypocrisy, to flattery, and even to hiding his own lack of understanding, for biographical truth is not to be had, and even if it were it couldn't be used.

Sigmund Freud, in a letter to Arnold Zweig, *who had suggested being his biographer.* •292

Oh, fond attempt to give a deathless lot
To names ignoble, born to be forgot!

William Cowper, On Observing Some Names of Little Note Recorded in the Biographia Britannica *(1782)* •293

I have decided to keep a full journal, in the hope that my life will perhaps seem more interesting when it is written down.
Sue Townsend, in Adrian Mole: The Wildnerness Years *(1993)* •294

It's the good girls who keep the diaries. The bad girls never have the time.
Tallulah Bankhead •295

What is more dull than a discreet diary? One might just as well have a discreet soul.
Henry Chips Channon, Diary, *26 July 1935* •296

I never travel without my diary. One should always have something sensational to read on the train.
Oscar Wilde, The Importance of Being Earnest *(1895)* •297

Autobiography is probably the most respectable form of lying.
Humphrey Carpenter, Patrick White Explains Himself, *in* The New York Times Book Review *7 February 1982* •298

An Autobiography is an obituary in serial form with the last instalment missing.
Quentin Crisp, The Naked Civil Servant, *1968.*
•299

Theres no such thing as autobiography. There's only art and lies.
Jeanette Winterson in The Guardian, *5 July 1994* •301

Autobiographies tell more lies than all but the most self-indulgent fiction.

A.S. Byatt, Sugar *(1988)* •300

Only when one has lost all curiosity about the future has one reached the age to write an autobiography.

Evelyn Waugh,
A Little Learning *(1964)* •302

The one essential part of all my education.

John Ruskin, of his daily Bible readings with his mother; in Dictionary of National Biography. •303

I walk many times into the pleasant fields of the Holy Scriptures, where I pluck up the goodly green herbs of sentences, eat them by reading, chew them up musing, and lay them up at length in the seat of memory… so I may less perceive the bitterness of this miserable life.

Elizabeth I, in Adam Fox (ed.) A Book of Devotions *(1970)* •305

You cannot name any example in any heathen author but I will better it in Scripture.

James I, in Thomas Overbury (1581-1613), 'Crumms Fal'n From King James's Table' published 1715 •304

Never forget, gentlemen, never forget that this is not the Bible. This, gentlemen, is only a translation of the Bible.

Richard Whately to a meeting of his diocesan clergy, as he held up a copy of the 'Authorized Version'. *In* H. Solly, These Eighty Years *(1893)* •306

Translation it is that openeth
the window, to let in the light;
that breaketh the shell,
that we may eat the kernel;
that putteth aside the curtain,
that we may look into the most
holy place; that removeth
the cover of the well, that
we may come by the water.
Bible, Authorized Version *(1611)* '
The Translators to the Reader' •307

There's a Bible on that shelf
there. But I keep it next to
Voltaire — poison and antidote.
Bertrand Russell, in **Kenneth Harris**
Talking To Bertrand Russell, *1971* •308

I read the book of Job last night.
I don't think God comes well out of it.
Virginia Woolf, **letter to Lady Robert Cecil,**
12 November 1922 •309

77

Literature is the question
minus the answer.

Roland Barthes, in
New York Times *1978* •310

Classic. A book
which people praise
and don't read.

Mark Twain, Following the Equator
(1897) •312

Great literature is simply
language charged with
meaning to the utmost
possible degree.

Ezra Pound, How To Read *(1931)* •311

A classic is something that
everybody wants to read.

Mark Twain, The Disappearance of
Literature, *1900* •313

Definition of a classic:
a book everyone is assumed
to have read and often
thinks they have.

Alan Bennett, **Independent on Sunday,**
1991 •314

Literature is the art of
writing something
that will be read twice;
journalism what will
be read once.

Cyril Connolly,
Enemies of Promise *(1938)* •315

The virtue of much literature
is that it is dangerous and
may do you extreme harm.

John Mortimer, in C.H. Rolph, Books in
the Dock *(1969)* •316

You're familiar with the
tragedies of antiquity,
are you? The great
homicidal classics?

Tom Stoppard, **Rosencrantz and
Guildenstern are Dead** *(1967)* •317

A man with a
belly full of the
classics is an enemy
of the human race.

Henry Miller, **Tropic of Cancer,** *1930* •318

And now I have finished
the work, which neither
the wrath of Jove, nor
fire, nor the sword, nor
devouring age shall be
able to destroy.

Ovid, Metamorphoses •319

A classic is a
book that has
never finished
saying what it
has to say.

Italo Calvino, The Literature
Machine *(1987)* •320

Literature is a luxury; fiction is a necessity.

G.K. Chesterton, The Defendants *(1901)*
A Defence of Penny Dreadfuls •321

Fiction is to the grown man what play is to the child; it is there that he changes the atmosphere and tenor of his life.

Robert Louis Stevenson,
Memories and Portraits *(1887)* •322

There is no longer any such thing as fiction or non-fiction; there's only narrative.

E.L. Doctorow, in New York Times
Book Review *27 January 1988* •323

Fiction is like a spider's web, attached ever so lightly perhaps, but still attached to life at all four corners. *Virginia Woolf* •324

I abhor a mystery. I would fain, were it possible, have my tale run through from its little prologue to its customary marriage in its last chapter, with all the smoothness incidental to ordinary life. I have no ambition to surprise my reader.

Anthony Trollope,
The Bertrams *(1859)* •325

The key to a short story is tension. At the start of a short story the reader's imagination should be able to take the story on in his mind, but at the end of a novel he is entitled to expect a rounding-off.

William Trevor, interview in
Sunday Telegraph *21 January 1990* •326

The novel tends to tell us everything, whereas the short story tells us only one thing, and that intensely.

V.S. Pritchett, **attrib.** •327

No human being ever spoke of scenery for above two minutes at a time, which makes me suspect we hear too much of it in literature.

Robert Louis Stevenson,
Memories and Portraits *(1887)* •328

To illustrate any text is also to interpret it.

Pulitzer prize-winning writer and scholar
Alison Lurie, Don't Tell the Grown-Ups
(1990) •329

Illustration is a very old form, far older than the novel, balanced somewhere in between painting and literature but belonging to neither.

Childrens author and illustrator Shirley Hughes, A Life Drawing *(2002)* •330

The good ended happily, and the bad unhappily. That is what fiction means.

Oscar Wilde, The Importance of Being Earnest *(1895)* •331

What the detective story is about is not murder but the restoration of order.

P.D. James, in Face, *December 1986* •332

Detection is, or ought to be, an exact science, and should be treated in the same cold and unemotional manner. You have attempted to tinge it with romanticism, which produces much the same effect as if you worked a love-story or an elopement into the fifth proposition of Euclid.

Arthur Conan Doyle, Sherlock Holmes in The Sign of Four *(1890)* •333

There were no innocent blondes in crime fiction.

Ed McBain, on writing for crime magazines, in Writers on Writing: Collected Essays from the New York Times *(2001)* •334

83

How are we to account for the strange human craving for the pleasure of feeling afraid which is so much involved in our love of ghost stories?

Virginia Woolf, in The Times Literary Supplement 'Across the Border' *(1918)* •335

The tale of terror, like pornography, with which it has much in common, represents a carefree holiday from ethics.

Angela Carter, in New Society *1975* •336

Terror... often arises from a pervasive sense of disestablishment; that things are in the unmaking.

Stephen King, Danse Macabre *(1981)* •337

[The ghost story is] certainly the most exacting form of literary art, and perhaps the only one in which there is no immediate step between success and failure. Either it comes off or it is a flop.

L.P. Hartley in Cynthia Asquith (ed.) The Third Ghost Book *(1955)* Introduction
•338

Where there is no imagination there is no horror.

Arthur Conan Doyle, A Study in Scarlet *(1888)* •339

We like to think we live in daylight, but half the world is always dark; and fantasy, like poetry, speaks the language of the night.

Ursula Le Guin, in World Magazine *21 November 1979* •340

It is fortunate for tale-tellers that they are not tied down like theatrical writers to the unities of time and place.

Sir Walter Scott, **Tales of My Landlord 1st series,** *(1816)* **Old Mortality** •341

If some fatal process of applied science enables us in fact to reach the moon, the real journey will not at all satisfy the impulse which we now seek to gratify by writing such stories.

C.S. Lewis, **Of Other Worlds** *(1966)* •342

We need metaphors of magic and monsters in order to understand the human condition.

Stephen Donaldson •343

Bingo Bolger-Baggins; a bad name. Let Bingo = Frodo.

J.R.R. Tolkien does some reworking on the first draft of Lord of the Rings; *note c. 1938, cited in* **Humphrey Carpenter, J.R.R. Tolkien** *(1977)* •344

Most modern fantasy just rearranges the furniture in Tolkien's attic.

Terry Pratchett, in **Stan Nicholls (ed.) Wordsmiths of Wonder** *(1993)* •345

Don't read science fiction books. It'll look bad if you die in bed with one on the nightstand. Always read stuff that will make you look good if you die in the middle of the night.

P.J. ORourke, **attrib.** *1979* •346

85

Do you ever read what they call Science Fiction? It's a scream. It's written like this: I checked out with K19 on Adabaran III, and stepped out through the crummaliote hatch on my 22 Model Sirius Hardtop. I cocked the timejector in secondary and waded through the bright blue manda grass. My breath froze into pink pretzels. I flicked on the heat bars and the Bryllis ran swiftly on five legs using their other two to send out crylon vibrations…

Raymond Chandler, **letter to H.N. Swanson,** *14 March 1953* •347

We live in a world where emissions from our refrigerators have caused the ozone layer to evaporate and now we'll get skin cancer if we sunbathe. If that's not a science fiction scenario, I don't know what is.

William Gibson, **Perspectives** *in* **Newsweek,** *5 June 1995* •348

What is the use of a book, thought Alice, without pictures or conversations?

Lewis Carroll, **Alice's Adventures in Wonderland** *(1865)* •349

Victorian children's stories are full of children who cannot read anywhere except in a deeply embrasured window seat.

Robertson Davies, **lecture, Yale** *20 February 1990* •350

It may be better for them to read some things, especially fairy stories, that are beyond their measure rather than short of it. Their books like their clothes should allow for growth, and their books at any rate should encourage it.

J.R.R. Tolkien on literature for children, **Tree and Leaf** *(1964)* **On Fairy-Stories** •351

Satire is a sort of glass, wherein beholders do generally discover everybody's face but their own; which is the chief reason for that kind of reception it meets in the world, and that so very few are offended with it.
Jonathan Swift, **The Battle of the Books** *(1704),* **preface** •352

Writing about travels is nearly always tedious, travelling being, like war and fornication, exciting but not interesting.
Malcolm Muggeridge, in **Observer** *5 September 1976* •353

And what's romance? Usually, a nice little tale where you have everything As You Like It, where rain never wets your jacket and gnats never bite your nose and it's always daisy-time.
D.H. Lawrence, **Studies in Classic American Literature** *(1924)* •354

I have no problem with chick lit, I love Bridget Jones's Diary, it's just great. It's all the muck in the middle I mind... Let's have art or let's have entertainment.
Jeanette Winterson, in **BBC News (online edition)** *23 August 2001* •355

'I am fond of history'.
'I wish I were too. I read it a little as a duty, but it tells me nothing that does not vex or weary me. The quarrels of popes and kings, with wars and pestilences, in every page; the men all so good for nothing, and hardly any women at all.' *Jane Austen,* **Northanger Abbey** *(1818)* •356

It has been said that though God cannot alter the past, historians can; it is perhaps because they can be useful to Him in this respect that He tolerates their existence. *Samuel Butler,* **Erewhon Revisited** *(1901)* •357

Tragedy is like strong acid — it dissolves away all but the very gold of truth. *D.H. Lawrence,* **letter,** *1 April 1911* •359

Whosoever, in writing a history, shall follow truth too near the heels, it may happily strike out his teeth. *Walter Ralegh,* The History of the World *(1614)* •358

Comedy is tragedy that happens to other people. *Angela Carter,* **Wise Children** *(1991)* •360

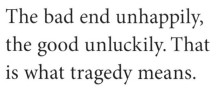

The bad end unhappily, the good unluckily. That is what tragedy means.

Tom Stoppard, Rosencrantz and Guildenstern are Dead *(1967)* •361

Theatre is recreation. It can be much more, but unless it's recreation, I don't see the point of it. *Tom Stoppard, in* Village Voice, *4 April 1995* •362

A play, I think, ought to make sense to commonsense people. Drama is akin to other inventions of man in that it ought to help us know more, and not merely to spend our feelings.
Arthur Miller (with regard to his play The Crucible), attrib. •363

I've never much enjoyed going to plays… The unreality of painted people standing on a platform saying things they've said to each other for months is more than I can overlook.
John Updike, in George Plimpton (ed.) Writers at Work 4th Series *(1977)* •364

I consider it injurious for a dramatic work to be first made available to the public by a stage performance… [because it] can never be judged and understood in isolation as a piece of literature. Judgement will always include both the piece and its performance.
Henrik Ibsen, letter *1872* •365

Show me a congenital eavesdropper with the instincts of a Peeping Tom and I will show you the makings of a dramatist. *Kenneth Tynan,* **Pausing on the Stairs,** *1957* •366

At least one of my children did one of my plays at A-level. I think he got a 'B' with my help.
Tom Stoppard on being a 'set text' author; attrib. 1995 •367

A bad experience of Shakespeare is like a bad oyster — it puts you off for life. *Judi Dench* •368

The play was a great success, but the audience was a total failure.

Oscar Wilde after the first performance of **Lady Windermere's Fan,** *in Peter Hay,* **Theatrical Anecdotes** *(1987)* •369

Poetry's a mere drug, Sir.

George Farquhar, Love and a Bottle *(1698))*•370

Poetry is devil's wine.

St. Augustine, **Contra Academicos** •373

So poetry is something more
philosophical and more worthy
of serious attention than history,
for while poetry is concerned
with universal truths, history
treats of particular facts.

Aristotle, **Poetics** •371

Nature never set forth the earth
in so rich tapestry as diverse poets
have done… her world is brazen,
the poets only deliver a golden.

Philip Sidney, **The Defence of Poetry**
(1595)•374

No verse can give
pleasure for long,
nor last, that is written
by drinkers of water.

Horace, **Epistles.** •372

So long as men can breathe,
  or eyes can see,
So long lives this, and this
  gives life to thee.

William Shakespeare, **Sonnet 18** •375

For rhyme the rudder is
  of verses,

With which like ships they
  steer their courses.

Samuel Butler, **Hudibras pt.1** *(1663)* •376

The troublesome and modern bondage of rhyming. *John Milton,* **Paradise Lost** *(1667)* **The Verse** *(Preface, added 1668)* •377

Boswell: What is poetry?
Johnson: Why Sir, it is much easier to say what it is not. We all *know* what light is; but it is not easy to *tell* what it is.

Samuel Johnson, **Boswell, Life of Samuel Johnson** *(1791) 12 April 1776* •378

You will never be alone with a poet in your pocket.

John Adams, **letter to John Quincy Adams,** *14 May 1781* •379

Poetry, indeed, cannot be translated; and, therefore, it is poets that preserve languages; for we would not be at the trouble to learn a language, if we could have all that is written in it just as well in translation. But as the beauties of poetry cannot be preserved in any language except that in which it was originally written, we learn the language.

Samuel Johnson, in **James Boswell, Life of Samuel Johnson** *(1791)* •380

Poetry is the spontaneous overflow of powerful feelings: it takes its origin from emotion recollected in tranquility.

William Wordsworth, **Lyrical Ballads** *(2nd ed. 1802* •381

Poetry is thoughts that breathe,
and words that burn.
Thomas Gray •382

Whither is fled the
visionary gleam?
Where is it now, the
glory and the dream?

**William Wordsworth, Ode. Intimations
of Immortality** *(1807)* •383

If poetry comes not
as naturally as the leaves
to a tree it had better
not come at all.

John Keats, **letter to John Taylor,**
27 February 1818 •384

Poetry should surprise by a fine excess,
and not by a singularity — it should
strike the reader as a wording of his
own highest thoughts, and appear
almost a remembrance.

John Keats, **letter to John Taylor,**
27 February 1818 •385

Poetry is the record of the best
and happiest moments of the
happiest and best minds.

Percy Bysshe Shelley, **A Defence
of Poetry** *(written 1821)* •386

Prose = words in their best
order; — poetry = the best
words in the best order.

Samuel Taylor Coleridge, **Table Talk**
(1835), 12 July 1827 •387

Everything you invent is true: you can be sure of that. Poetry is a subject as precise as geometry. *Gustave Flaubert,* **letter to Louise Colet,** *14 August 1853* •388

Prose wanders around with a lantern and laboriously schedules and verifies the details and particulars of a valley and its frame of crags and peaks, then Poetry comes, and lays bare the whole landscape with a single splendid flash. *Mark Twain; in* **H.N. Smith and W.H. Gibson (eds.) Mark Twain-Howells Letters vol. 2** *(1960)* •389

Poetry is the opening and closing of a door, leaving those who look through to guess about what is seen during a moment. *Carl Sandburg, in* **Atlantic Monthly** *March 1923* •390

We make out of the quarrel with others, rhetoric, but of the quarrel with ourselves, poetry. *W.B. Yeats,* **Essays** *(1924)* **'Anima Hominis'** •391

A poem should not mean But be. *Archibald MacLeish,* **Ars Poetica** *(1926)* •392

Genuine poetry can communicate before it is understood. *T.S. Eliot,* **Dante** *(1929)* •393

As soon as war is declared it will be impossible to hold the poets back. Rhyme is still the most effective drum.

Jean Giraudoux, **La Guerre de Troie n'aura pas lieu** *(1935)* •394

Writing free verse is like playing tennis with the net down.

Robert Frost, speech at Milton Academy, Massachusetts, 1935. •395

Publishing a volume of poetry is like dropping a rose petal down the Grand Canyon and waiting for the echo.

Don Marquis, **Sun Dial Time** *(1936)* •396

An age which is incapable of poetry is incapable of any kind of literature except the cleverness of a decadence.

Raymond Chandler, **letter to Charles W. Morton,** *5 January 1947* •397

[Poetry] is a violence from within that protects us from a violence without.

Wallace Stevens, **The Noble Rider And The Sounds of Words** *(1951)* •398

Poetry is sissy stuff that rhymes. Weedy people sa la and fie and swoon when they see a bunch of daffodils.

Geoffrey Willans and Ronald Searle, **Down With Skool!** *(1953)* •399

Prose is when all the lines except the last go on to the end. Poetry is when some of them fall short of it.

Jeremy Bentham, in M. St. J. Packe, The Life of John Stuart Mill *(1954)* •400

Poetry should begin with emotion in the poet, and end with the same emotion in the reader. The poem is simply the instrument of transference.

Philip Larkin, BBC Third Programme, *13 April 1956* •401

The crown of literature is poetry. It is its end and aim. It is the sublimest activity of the human mind. It is the achievement of beauty and delicacy. The writer of prose can only step aside when the poet passes.

W. Somerset Maugham, Saturday Review, *1957* •402

Poetry is so emotional and very tiring.

Edith Sitwell, attrib. *(1957)* •403

Poetry is the revelation of a feeling that the poet believes to be interior and personal but which the reader recognizes as his own.*Salvatore Quasimodo, in* New York Times *14 May 1960* •404

Most people ignore most poetry because most poetry ignores most people.
Adrian Mitchell, Poems *(1964)* •405

My favourite poem is the one that starts 'Thirty days has September' because it actually tells you something.

Groucho Marx, in **Ned Sherrin, Cutting Edge** *(1984)* **attrib.** •406

Poetry is to prose as dancing is to walking.

John Wain, talk on **BBC Radio,** *1976* •407

Novels are about other people and poems are about yourself.

Philip Larkin, **Required Writing** *(1983)* •408

I don't know why I bother really, because people don't listen to lyrics in rock'n'roll records too much.

Lou Reed, 1989 •409

I have emotion — no one who knows me could fail to detect it

But there's a serious shortage of tranquillity in which to recollect it.

So this is my contribution to the theoretical debate:

Sometimes poetry is emotion recollected in a highly emotional state.

Wendy Cope, **An Argument with Wordsworth** *(1992)* •410

Metrical poetry is ultimately allied to song, and I like the connection. Free verse is ultimately allied to conversation, and I like that connection too

Thom Gunn, in **Paris Review** *1995* •411

98

Often what a poet does not say
is as important as what he does.

*Miroslav Holub at a reading in Prague
of Seamus Heaney's poetry,* April 1996; *in*
The Sunday Times *28 April 1996* •412

There are poems about
the Internet and about
the shipping forecast
but very few by women
celebrating men.

*Germaine Greer addressing
the Poetry Society.* •413

Poetry is not the most
important thing in life…
I'd much rather lie in a
hot bath reading Agatha
Christie and sucking sweets.

Dylan Thomas, in Joan Wyndham Love is
Blue *(1986) 6 July 1943* •414

All poets are mad.

Robert Burton, The Anatomy of Melancholy
(1621-51), **'Democritus to the Reader'** •415

I am obnoxious to each
  carping tongue,
Who says my hand a needle
  better fits,
A poet's pen, all scorn, I should
  thus wrong;
For such despite they cast on
  female wits:
If what I do prove well, it
  won't advance,
They'll say it's stolen, or else it
  was by chance.

Anne Bradstreet, The Prologue *(1650)* •416

Some rhyme a neebor's name
  to lash;
Some rhyme (vain thought!) for
  needfu' cash;
Some rhyme to court the
  countra clash,
An' raise a din;
For me, an aim I never fash;
  I rhyme for fun.

Robert Burns, To J.S[mith] *(1786)* •417

The reason Milton wrote
in fetters when he wrote
of Angels and God, and at
liberty when of Devils and
Hell, is because he was a true
Poet, and of the Devil's party
without knowing it.

William Blake, The Marriage
of Heaven and Hell *(1790-3)* •418

Poets are the unacknowledged legislators of the world.

Percy Bysshe Shelley, **A Defence of Poetry** *(written 1821)* •419

The poets are full of false views: they make mankind believe that happiness consists in falling in love, and living in the country. I say: live in London; like many people; fall in love with nobody.

Sydney Smith, **letter to Lady Dacre,** *1837* •420

It is beautiful; it is mournful; it is monotonous.

Charlotte Brontë on Tennyson's **In Memoriam; letter to Mrs Gaskell,** *27 August 1850* •421

Do I contradict myself?
Very well then I contradict myself,
(I am large, I contain multitudes).

Walt Whitman, **Song of Myself** *(written 1855)* •422

Wordsworth went to the Lakes, but he never was a lake poet.. He found in stones the sermons he had already put there.

Oscar Wilde on William Wordsworth •423

We have been able to have
fine poetry in England because
the public do not read it, and
consequently do not influence it.
The public like to insult poets
because they are individual, but
once they have insulted them,
they leave them alone.

Oscar Wilde, The Soul of Man
under Socialism, *1891* •424

All things can tempt me
from this craft of verse.

W.B. Yeats, All Things Can Tempt Me *(1909)*
•425

All a poet can
do today is warn.

First World War poet Wilfred Owen,
Preface *(written 1918),* Poems *(1963)* •426

Words in search of a meaning.

Roman Jakobson, The Newest Russian
Poetry *(1919; revised 1921)* •427

Immature poets imitate;
mature poets steal.

T.S. Eliot, The Sacred Wood *(1920)*
Philip Massinger •428

Tennyson and Browning
are poets, and they think;
but they do not feel their
thought as immediately
as the odour of a rose.
A thought to Donne
was an experience; it
modified his sensibility.

T.S. Eliot, The Metaphysical Poets *(1921)* •429

I am a freak user of words, not a poet. That's really the truth.

Dylan Thomas, **letter** *9 May 1934* •430

There was a little about melancholia that he didn't know; there was little else that he did.

W.H. Auden on Alfred, Lord Tennyson; **introduction to A Selection From the Poems of Alfred, Lord Tennyson** *(1947)* •431

I am a painstaking, conscientious, involved and devious craftsman in words… I use everything to make my poems work and move in the directions I want them to: old tricks, new tricks, puns, portmanteau-words, paradox, allusion, paranomasia, paragram, catachesis, slang, assonantal rhymes, vowel rhymes, sprung rhythm…Poets have got to enjoy themselves sometimes.

Dylan Thomas, **Poetic Manifesto** *(1951)* •432

I should say that Milton's experience of propaganda is what makes his later poetry so very dramatic; that is, though he is a furious partisan, he can always imagine with all its force exactly what the reply of the opponent would be.

William Empson, **Milton's God** *(1961)* •433

The Rabbie Burns of England.
James Knox, on John Betjeman •434

A poet's hope: to be,
like some valley cheese,
local, but prized elsewhere.
W.H. Auden, **Shorts II** *(1976)* •435

When I get sent manuscripts
from aspiring poets, I do one
of two things: if there is no stamp
self-addressed envelope, I throw
it into the bin. If there is, I write
and tell them to fuck off.

Philip Larkin •436

I very much feel the need to be on the periphery of things.

Philip Larkin, in **Observer** *16 December 1979*
•437

Hughes's voice, I think, is in rebellion against a
certain kind of demeaned, mannerly voice… the
Larkin voice, the Movement voice, even the Eliot
voice, the Auden voice – the manners of that
speech, the original voices behind that poetic
voice, are those of literate middle-class culture,
and I think Hughes's great cry and call and bawl
is that English language and English poetry is
longer and deeper than that.
Seamus Heaney, in **John Haffendn** (ed.)
Viewpoints *(1981)* •438

I would have a poet able-bodied,
fond of talking, a reader of the
newspapers, capable of pity and
laughter, informed in economics,
appreciative of women, involved
in personal relationships, actively
interested in politics, susceptible
to physical impressions.
Louis MacNeice, **Modern Poetry** *(1938)* •439

She wrote her early poems very slowly, thesaurus open on her knee... chewing her lips, putting a thick dark ring of ink around each word that stirred her on the page of the thesaurus.

Ted Hughes on his wife Sylvia Plath, in **Seamus Heaney, Finders Keepers** *(2002)* •440

The only poets with full-time salaries earn them at greeting-card companies.

Bill Thomas, in **Los Angeles Times** *13 January 1991* •441

In no other job have I ever had to deal with such utterly abnormal people. Yes, it is true, poetry does something to them.

Muriel Spark, on working for the Poetry Society; **Curriculum Vitae** *(1992)* •442

The poetry world is very small and full of green-eyed snapping fish.

Andrew Motion •443

Poets or artists are sometimes married very happily to their muse; and sometimes they have a very difficult life with her.

W.H. Auden, in conversation with Isaiah Berlin, **Daily Telegraph** *3 August 1996* •444

I used think all poets were Byronic —
mad, bad and dangerous to know.
And then I met a few.
They're mostly wicked as ginless
tonic and wild as pension plans.

Wendy Cope •445

People ask you for criticism, but they only want praise.

W. Somerset Maugham,
Of Human Bondage *(1915)* •446

Whom the Gods wish to destroy they first call promising.

Cyril Connolly, **Enemies of Promise,** *1938* •447

Criticism is a study by which men grow important and formidable at very small expense.

Samuel Johnson, in The Idler
9 June 1759 •448

People who like this sort of thing will find this the sort of thing they like.

Abraham Lincoln's judgement of a book, in
G.W.E. Russell, Collections and Recollections
(1898) •449

If they [writers] believe the critics when they say they are great then they must believe them when they say they are rotten and they lose confidence.

Ernest Hemingway, Green Hills of Africa
(1935) •450

I am strongly of the opinion that an author had far better not read any reviews of his books: the unfavourable ones are almost certain to make him cross, and the favourable ones conceited; and neither of these results is desirable.

Lewis Carroll, Sylvie and Bruno Concluded
(1893) •451

They [writers] fret over savage reviews because rejection of their work… means rejection of themselves and of their working lives… However, it is clear that no review, no matter how bad or how unfair, can seriously injure the sales of a book if the public desires to read it.
Irving Wallace, The Writing of One Novel *(1968)* •452

There's no such thing as bad publicity except your own obituary.
Brendan Behan, Irish playwright, in **Dominic Behan, My Brother Brendan** *(1965)* •453

If it is abuse, — why one is always sure to hear of it from one damned good natured friend or another!
Richard Brinsley Sheridan, **The Critic** *(1779)* •454

It is the nature of the artist to mind excessively what is said about him. Literature is strewn with the wreckage of men who have minded beyond reason the opinions of others. *Virginia Woolf,* **A Room of One's Own,** *1929* •455

No critical display is more offensive than that which praises one author by damning another, as though critical judgement were a seesaw on which one reputation cannot rise unless another is lowered.
Carolyn G. Heilbrun, **Hamlet's Mother and Other Women** *(1990)* 'Virginia Woolf and James Joyce' •456

109

With all those prizes the most interesting thing is getting on the shortlist, because that tells you who people see as your peers.

David Malouf, in The Daily Telegraph, *7 September 1996* •457

I will try to account for the degree of my aesthetic emotion. That, I conceive, is the function of the critic.

Clive Bell, Art *(1914)* •458

That one book is better than another is nothing more than a matter of taste. I find it difficult to accept that it's something that can be decided by a panel of judges.

Graham Swift, in The Observer *24 June 1990 'Sayings of the Week'* •459

This is an important book, the critic assumes, because it deals with war. This is an insignificant book because it deals with the feelings of women in a drawing-room.

Virginia Woolf, A Room of One's Own *(1929)* •460

The whole idea of an award just for women fills me with horror.

Anita Brookner voices her opposition to the Orange Prize for women's fiction, in The Sunday Times *21 April 1996* •461

Some of the editors wrote rejection slips that were more creative than anything I had written. On my tenth submission to Redbook… 'Mrs Clark, your stories are light, slight, and trite.' My first novella was returned with the succinct note: 'We found the heroine as boring as her husband had.'

Mary Higgins Clark, in The Writing Life: Collection from Washington Post Book World *(2003)* •462

You may abuse a tragedy, though you cannot write one. You may scold a carpenter who has made you a bad table, though you cannot make a table. It is not your trade to make tables.

Samuel Johnson, in James Boswell, Life of Samuel Johnson *(1791)*
25 June 1763 •463

Every genius needs praise.

Gertrude Stein, in Edmund White,
The Burning Library *(1994)*•464

A critic is a man who knows the way but can't drive the car.

Kenneth Tynan, in New York Times Magazine *9 January 1966* •465

Criticism is a life without risk.
John Lahr, Light Fantastic *(1996)* •467

There is, perhaps, no more dangerous man in the world than the man with the sensibilities of an artist but without creative talent. With luck such men make wonderful theatrical impresarios and interior decorators, or else they become mass murderers or critics.

Barry Humphries, More Please *(1992)* •466

A man is a critic when he cannot be an artist, in the same way that a man becomes an informer when he cannot be a soldier.

Gustave Flaubert, letter to Louise Colet *(1846)* •468

113

A good writer is not
per se a good book critic.
No more than a good drunk
is automatically a good
bartender. *Jim Bishop, in*
New York Journal,
November 1957 •469

A true critic ought to dwell
rather upon excellencies than
imperfections, to discover the
concealed beauties of a writer,
and communicate to the world
such things as are worth their
observation. *Joseph Addison,*
The Spectator
2 February 1712 •470

A sneer of critics.

Peter Nichols coins a collective noun,
Diary *6 February 1974* •471

Western man, especially the
Western critic, still finds it
very hard to go into print and
say: 'I recommend you go to
see this because it gave me
an erection'. *Kenneth Tynan,*
Playboy, *1977* •472

Though it often apes scientific language,
critical theory would not be recognised
as theory by any scientist, since it does
not open itself up to experimental
verification. Composed purely of
assertions, not testable hypotheses,
it can have no bearing on reality,
and no explanatory value.
John Carey, in The Sunday Times
7 August 1994 •473

I never read
a book before
reviewing it;
it prejudices
a man so.

Sydney Smith, in H. Pearson,
The Smith of Smiths *(1934)* •474

Asking a playwright
how he felt about
critics was like
asking a lamppost
how it felt about dogs.

Christopher Hampton, in
The Times *4 April 1995* •475

He was not of an age,
but for all time!
Ben Jonson, **To the Memory of
My Beloved, the Author, Mr
William Shakespeare** *(1623)* •476

In his plays you often
find remarks doing a
kitchen-hand's work
in some remote corner
of a sentence which
would deserve pride of
place in a disquisition
by any other writer.
Georg Christoph Lichtenberg,
notebooks *1765-99* •477

Was there ever such stuff as
a great part of Shakespeare?
Only one must not say so!
But what think you? — what?
— Is there not sad stuff?
what — what? *George III,
to Fanny Burney,*
Diary, *19 December 1785* •478

It is said that Shakespeare depicted
the Romans superbly. I don't see
this. They are sheer, inveterate
Englishmen, but they are truly human,
fundamentally human, and so the
Roman toga suits them well enough.
Johann Wolfgang von Goethe, **Shakespeare
without End** *(1815)* •479

He was not a man, he was
a continent; he contained
whole crowds of men,
entire landscapes.
Gustave Flaubert on Shakespeare,
letter, *19 September 1852* •480

Fantastic! And it
was all written
with a feather!

*American film producer Sam Goldwyn
on the works of Shakespeare;* attrib.,
in **John Gross, After Shakespeare** *(2002)* •481

The remarkable thing about Shakespeare is that he really is very good, in spite of all the people who say he is very good.
Robert Graves, 1964 •482

There is a sense in which every writer in English owes a debt to Shakespeare. He is our theatrical DNA.
Richard Eyre, **Changing Stages, BBC2 TV,** *5 November 2000* •483

To escape from the grotesque tragedy which was his body, Pope perfected a series of immaculate masks and voices.
John Carey, in **The Sunday Times** *1985* •484

This man… who has the most extensive knowledge, the clearest understanding, and the greatest abilities of any living author, — has a face the most ugly, a person the most awkward, and manners the most singular, that ever were, or ever can be seen. But all that is unfortunate in his exterior, is so greatly compensated for in his interior, that I can only, like Desdemona to Othello, 'see his visage in his mind'. *Fanny Burney, of Samuel Johnson,* **letter to her sister Susan,** *August 1778* •485

I am in the path of Blake, but so far behind him that only the wings of his heels are in sight.
Dylan Thomas, **letter to Pamela Hansford Johnson,** *undated, probably September 1933* •486

He talked on for ever; and you wished him to talk on for ever.
William Hazlitt on Coleridge, **Lectures on the English Poets** *(1818)* •487

The owner of a mind which keeps open house, and entertains all comers.

William Hazlitt on Coleridge,
The Spirit of the Age *(1825)* •488

Walter Scott has no business to write novels, especially good ones — It is not fair. — He has fame and profit enough as a poet, and should not be taking the bread out of other people's mouths. — I do not like him, and do not mean to like Waverley if I can help it — but fear I must. *Jane Austen,* **letter to Anna Austen,** *28 September 1814* •489

The Big Bow-Wow strain I can do myself like any now going; but the exquisite touch, which renders ordinary commonplace things and characters interesting, from the truth of the description and the sentiment, is denied to me.
Sir Walter Scott compares himself to Jane Austen, in W.E.K. Anderson (ed.), **Journals of Sir Walter Scott** *(1972) 14 March 1826* •490

Shelley is truth itself — and honour itself — notwithstanding his out-of-the-way notions about religion.
Lord Byron on Percy Bysshe Shelley, **letter to Douglas Kinnaird,** *2 June 1821* •491

Hair in disorder, eyes lost in a dream, a genius who, in his little room, is able to reconstruct bit by bit the entire structure of his society and to expose life in all its tumultuousness for his contemporaries and for all generations to come.

Auguste Rodin on Balzac, in
L'Art et les artistes, *February 1900* •492

Balzac observed all the things that Marx did not.

Régis Debray, **Teachers, Writers, Celebrities** *(1981)* 'Balzac, or Zoology Today' •493

He had a large loving mind and the strongest sympathy with the poorest classes. He felt sure a better feeling, and much greater union of classes, would take place in time. And I pray earnestly it may.

Queen Victoria, **Diary** *11 June 1870; on Charles Dickens.* •494

He describes London like a special correspondent for posterity. *Walter Bagehot, of Charles Dickens, in* **National Review** *7 October 1858,* '**Charles Dickens**' •495

My own experience in reading Dickens… is to be bounced between violent admiration and violent distaste almost every couple of paragraphs, and this is too uncomfortable a condition to be much alleviated by an inward recital of one's not to be fastidious, to gulp the stuff down in gobbets like a man.

Kingsley Amis, **What Became of Jane Austen?** *(1970)* •496

It does not matter that Dickens' world is not lifelike; it is alive.
Lord David Cecil, **Early Victorian Novelists** *(1978)* •497

We were put to Dickens as children but it never quite took. That unremitting humanity soon had me cheesed off.
Alan Bennett, **The Old Country** *(1978)* •498

Thackeray is like
the edited and
illustrated edition
of a great dinner.

Walter Bagehot, in Spectator *9 August 1862* •501

He remains in many ways
the foremost prophet of our
time…There is no one today
with Tolstoy's deep insight
and moral force.

Albert Einstein, interview in
Survey Graphic *August 1934* •499

His first, his inestimable
merit was a complete
appreciation of the usual.

Henry Jameson on Anthony Trollope,
Partial Portraits *(1888)* •502

He was as fond of me as
he could be of anyone
over the age of ten.

Ellen Terry on Lewis Carroll, in
Derek Hudson, Lewis Carroll •500

All modern American literature
comes from one book by Mark
Twain called Huckleberry Finn.

Ernest Hemingway, Green Hills of Africa *(1935)*
•503

Children swarmed to him like settlers. He became a land.

W.H. Auden on English artist and writer of humorous verse Edward Lear; **Edward Lear** *(1939)* •504

From the beginning Wilde performed his life and continued to do so even after fate had taken the plot out of his hands. *W.H. Auden, in* **New Yorker** *9 March 1963* •505

Chekhov made a mistake in thinking that if he had had more time he would have written more fully, described the rain, and the midwife and the doctor having tea. The truth is one can only get so much into a story; there is always a sacrifice. One has to leave out what one knows and longs to use.

Katherine Mansfield on fellow short story-writer Anton Chekhov, **Diary,** *1922* •506

I do not think Shaw will be a great literary figure in 2000AD. He is an amazingly brilliant contemporary; but he is not in the Hardy class.

Harold Nicolson, **Diary** *11 December 1950* •507

He is a most remarkable man — and I am the other one. Between us we cover all knowledge; he knows all that can be known and I know the rest.

Mark Twain, about Rudyard Kipling, **Autobiography** *(1924)* •508

121

Whatever Wells writes is not only alive, but kicking.

Henry James on English novelist H.G. Wells, in **G.K. Chesterton, Autobiography** *(1936)* •511

His virtuosity with language is not unlike that of one of his drill sergeants with an awkward squad… The vulgarest words learn to wash behind their ears and to execute complicated movements at the word of command, but they can hardly be said to learn to think for themselves.

W.H. Auden, re Kipling, in **New Republic** *24 October 1943* •509

He's the Shakespeare of science fiction.

Brian Aldiss on H.G. Wells, on **Bookmark** **(BBC2)** *24 August 1996* •512

One could always baffle Conrad by saying 'humour'. It was one of our damned English tricks he had never learned to tackle.

H.G. Wells on Joseph Conrad •510

Chesterton had a body like a slag heap, but a mind like the dawn sky. He saw the world new, as if he'd just landed from another planet.

John Carey, in **The Sunday Times** *1978* •513

An essentially private man, who wished his total indifference to public notice to be universally recognised. *Tom Stoppard on James Joyce* •514

His writing is not about something. It is the thing itself.

Samuel Beckett, of James Joyce,
Our Examination Round His Factification
for Incamination of Work in Progress *(1929)*
•515

Few if any of the great novelists are people one would like to know as friends. Hemingway the bully; Proust the snob; Waugh the snobbish bully; Fitzgerald the drunk; Dickens the exhibitionist — they are all great novelists because they like to exploit and manipulate people, to mock and devastate people, to torment and trample on people — and we are talking, remember, of people they have themselves created.

Kenneth Tynan, Diary,
7 January 1972 •516

I was jealous of her writing — the only writing I have ever been jealous of.

Virginia Woolf, of Katherine Mansfield, shortly after the New Zealand writer's death; letter, *16 January 1923* •517

Kafka could never have written as he did had he lived in a house. His writing is that of someone whose whole life was spent in apartments, with lifts, stairwells, muffled voices behind closed doors, and sounds through walls. Put him in a nice detached villa and he'd never have written a word.
Alan Bennett on Czech novelist and short story writer Franz Kafka, **Writing Home** *(1994)* •518

Wherever one cut him, with a little question, he poured, spurted fountains of ideas.
Virginia Woolf on W.B. Yeats, **Diary,** *8 November 1930* •519

He wrote like God. He could put words together with such certainty that they seem to have been graven on tablets of stone from the beginning of time.
John Carey on W.B. Yeats; **Pure Pleasure** *(2000)* •520

Your novels beat me — black and blue… Of course I admire your creative work immensely — but only in a bemused and miserable manner.
Max Beerbohm, in a **letter to Virginia Woolf,** *30 December 1927* •521

I believe in the established canon of English and American literature and in the validity of the concept of privileged texts. I think it is more important to read Spenser, Shakespeare, or Milton than to read Borges in translation, or even, to say the truth, to read Virginia Woolf.
J. Hillis Miller, in **Sandra M. Gilbert, What Do Feminist Critics Want?** *(1980)* •522

You praise the firm restraint
  with which they write —
I'm with you there, of course:
They use the snaffle and the
  curb all right,
But where's the bloody horse?

Roy Campbell, 'On Some South African
Novelists' *(1930)* •523

An elderly fallen angel
travelling incognito.

*Peter Quennell on French novelist
and critic André Gide,* The Sign of
the Fish *(1960)* •524

As a man, he combines the
manner of Friar Tuck with
the mind of St. Augustine.

Kenneth Tynan on C.S. Lewis,
Persona Grata *(1953)* •525

Agatha Christie has given
more pleasure in bed than
any other woman.

Nancy Banks-Smith •526

He is a subtle poet, but
not a sophisticated one.

Philip Larkin on John Betjeman, Further
Requirements *(2001)* •527

Betjeman's cachet is by now that
of a cherished public monument.
It would be only mildly surprising
to hear that he had been acquired
by the National Trust.

John Carey, in The Sunday Times
9 January 1983 •528

He is both glum and funny,
a mixture the English
always find endearing.

John Carey on Alan Bennett, in
The Sunday Times *9 October 1994* •529

Coleridge was a drug addict.
Poe was an alcoholic.
Marlowe was stabbed by
a man whom he was
treacherously trying to stab.
Pope took money to keep
a woman's name out of a
satire then wrote a piece so
that she could be recognized
anyhow. Chatterton killed
himself. Byron was accused
of incest. Do you still want
to become a writer — and if
so, why? *Bennett Cerf,* Shake Well
Before Using *(1948)* •530

126

The Seven Ages Of Man

All the world's a stage,
And all the men and women merely players,
They have their exits and entrances,
And one man in his time plays many parts,
His acts being seven ages. At first the infant,
Mewling and puking in the nurse's arms.
  Then the whining schoolboy, with his satchel
And shining morning face, creeping like a snail
Unwillingly to school. And then the lover,
Sighing like furnace, with a woeful ballad
Made to his mistress' eyebrow.
Then a soldier, Full of strange oaths and
  bearded like the pard,
Jealous in honour, sudden and quick in quarrel,
Seeking the bubble reputation
Even in the cannon's mouth. And then
  the justice,
In fair round belly with good capon lined,
With eyes severe and beard of formal cut,
Full of wise saws and modern instances;
And so he plays his part. The sixth age shifts
Into the lean and slippered pantaloon,

With spectacles on nose and pouch on side,
His youthful hose, well saved, a world too wide,
For his shrunk shank; and his big manly voice,
Turning again towards the childish treble, pipes
And whistles in his sound. Last scene of all,
That ends this strange eventful history,
  Is second childishness and mere oblivion,
Sans teeth, sans eyes, sans taste,
  sans everything.

> *William Shakespeare,*
> **As You Like It,** *(1599)* II.vii •646

My mother groand! My father wept.
  Into the dangerous world I leapt:
Helpless, naked, piping loud:
  Like a fiend in a cloud.
Struggling in my father's hands:
  Striving against my swaddling bands:
Bound and weary I thought best
  To sulk upon my mother's breast.

William Blake, **Songs of Experience** *(1794)*
•647

In the dark womb
  where I began
My mother's life made
  me a man
        John Masefield, 'C.L.M', *(1910)* •648

I wish either my father or my mother,
or indeed both of them, as they were
in duty both equally bound to it, had
minded what they were about when
they begot me.   *Laurence Sterne,*
                Tristram Shandy *(1759-67)*
                •649

I s'pect I growed. Don't think nobody never made me.

Harriet Beecher Stowe, **Uncle Tom's Cabin**
(1852) — **said by Topsy** •650

If you really want to hear about it, the first thing
you'll probably want to know is where I was born,
and what my lousy childhood was like, and how
my parents were occupied before they had me,
and all that David Copperfield kind of crap.
**The opening lines of J.D. Salinger's
Catcher in the Rye** *(1920)* •651

Every baby born into the world is a finer one than the last.

Charles Dickens,
Nicholas Nickleby *(1839)* •652

Good work, Mary. We all knew you had it in you.

Dorothy Parker, in **a letter to Mrs Mary Sherwood on the arrival of her baby.** *In* **Alexander Woollcott, While Rome Burns,** *1934* •653

Our birth is but a sleep and
    a forgetting…

Not in entire forgetfulness,

And not in utter nakedness,

But trailing clouds of glory
    do we come.

> *William Wordsworth,* **Ode:
> Intimations of Immortality** *(1807)* •654

Love set you going like a
    fat gold watch.

The midwife slapped your footsoles,
    and your bald cry

Took its place among the elements.

Sylvia Plath, **'Morning Song',** *(1966)* •655

129

In every child who is born,
under no matter what
circumstances, and no
matter what parents, the
potentiality of the human
race is born again.

US novelist and poet James Agee,
Let Us Now Praise Famous Men *(1941)* •656

A bit of talcum
Is always walcum.

Ogden Nash, **Free Wheeling** *(1931)* •657

Sweet childish days,
  that were as long
As twenty days are now.
William Wordsworth, 'To a Butterfly' *(1807)*

•658

Behold the child, by Nature's
  kindly law
Pleased with a rattle, tickled
  with a straw.
Alexander Pope, An Essay on Man —
Epsitle 2 *(1733)* •659

Heaven lies about us in our infancy!

William Wordsworth,
'Ode. Intimations
of Immortality' *(1807)* •660

Childhood is not from birth to a
   certain age and at a certain age

The child is grown, and puts away
   childish things.

Childhood is the kingdom where
   nobody dies.

Nobody that matters, that is.

Edna St. Vincent Millay, **'Childhood is the
Kingdom where Nobody dies'** *(1934)* •661

The Child is Father of the Man

William Wordsworth, 'My heart leaps up
when I behold' •662

A decrepit father
   takes delight
To see his active child
   do deeds of youth.

William Shakespeare, Sonnet 37 •663

You are better than all the ballads,

That ever were sung or said;

For ye are living poems,

And all the rest are dead.

Henry Wadsworth Longfellow, **'Children'** •664

What music is
more enchanting
than the voices
of young people,
when you can't
hear what they say?

*Logan Pearsall Smith,
American essayist,* **Afterthoughts**
(1931) **'Age and Death'** •665

Children sweeten labours, but they make misfortunes more bitter.

Francis Bacon, Essays *(1625)* •666

The child that is not clean and neat,
With lots of toys and things to eat,
He is a naughty child, I'm sure —
Or else his dear papa is poor.

Robert Louis Stevenson, A Child's
Garden of Verses *(1885)* •668

It should be noted that children at play are not merely playing; their games should be seen as their most serious actions.

Montaigne, Essais *(1580)* •669

A child should always say
  what's true,
And speak when he is
  spoken to,
And behave mannerly at table:
At least as far as he is able.

Robert Louis Stevenson, A Child's
Garden of Verses *(1885)* •670

'Tis not good that children should know any wickedness.

William Shakespeare, The Merry Wives of
Windsor *(1597-8)* II.ii •671

It is only rarely that one can see in a little boy the promise of a man, but one can almost always see in a little girl the threat of a woman.

Alexandre Dumas (Fils); attrib. •672

Anybody who has survived his childhood has enough information about life to last him the rest of his days.

Flannery O'Connor, in New York Times Book Review, *1989* •673

The childhood shows the man, As morning shows the day.

Milton, Paradise Regained *(1671)* Book.4 •674

There is always one moment in childhood when the door opens and lets the future in.

Graham Greene, The Power and the Glory *(1940)* •675

134

For the hand that rocks the cradle
Is the hand that rules the world.
William Ross Wallace, **What Rules the World** *(1865)* •676

Children aren't happy
   with nothing to ignore,
And that's what parents
   were created for.

    Ogden Nash, 'The Parent', *(1933)* •677

Familiarity breeds contempt — and children.

Mark Twain, **Notebooks** *(1935)* •678

Childbirth was the moment of truth in my life. Suddenly you realise that you are having the greatest love affair of your life (but you also realise that God's a bloke).

Australian novelist Kathy Lette, in The Observer *June 1999* •679

What did my fingers do before
  they held him?
What did my heart do, with its love?
I have never seen a thing so clear.
His lids are like the lilac flower.
And soft as a moth, his breath.
I shall not let go.
There is no guile or warp in him.
  May he keep so.

Sylvia Plath, on seeing her newborn baby;
'Three Women: A Poem for Three Voices'
(1962) •680

Claudia… remembered that when she'd had her first baby she had realised with astonishment that the perfect couple consisted of a mother and child and not, as she had always supposed, a man and woman.

British writer Alice Thomas Ellis,
The Other Side of the Fire *(1983)* •681

Who ran to help me when I fell,
And would some pretty story tell,
Or kiss the place to make it well?
My Mother.

Ann Taylor and Jane Taylor,
'My Mother' (1804) •682

Few misfortunes can befall a boy which bring worse consequences than having a really affectionate mother.

W. Somerset Maugham, A Writer's Notebook, *written 1896,* pub. *1949* •683

What do girls do when they haven't any mothers to help them through their troubles?

Louisa May Alcott, **Little Women** *(1868)* •684

James James
Morrison Morrison
Weatherby George Dupree
Took great
Care of his Mother
Though he was only three.
James James
Said to his Mother,
'Mother,' he said, said he;
'You must never go down to the end
 of the town, if you don't go down
 with me'.

> *A.A. Milne,* **When We Were Very
> Young,** *(1924)* 'Disobedience' •685

It is not that I half knew my mother. I knew half of her — her lap, legs, feet, her hands and wrists as she bent forward.

Flann O'Brien, The Hard Life, *(1961)* •686

If I were damned of body and soul,

I know whose presence would
  make me whole,

Mother o' mine, O mother o' mine.

Rudyard Kipling, 'The Light That Failed' *(1891)*
•687

So for the mother's sake
  the child was dear,

And dearer was the
  mother for the child.

Coleridge, 'Sonnet to a Friend Who Asked
How I Felt When the Nurse First Presented
My Infant to Me' *(1797)* •688

I loved my parents (and I had more than the usual number to love).

Quentin Bell, of his biological parents Clive and Vanessa Bell, and Duncan Grant (father of his half-sister); in The Daily Telegraph *18 December 1996;* obituary •689

My wish was that my husband should be distinguished for intellect, and my children too. I have had my wish, — and I now wish that there was a little less intellect in the family so as to allow for a little more common sense.

Frances Rossetti, mother to William, Christina and Dante Gabriel; in William Rossetti (ed.) Dante Gabriel Rossetti: His Family Letters with a Memoir *(1895)* •690

A child is owed the greatest respect; if you ever have something disgraceful in mind, don't ignore your son's tender years.

Juvenal, Satires •691

It is a wise father that knows his own child.

William Shakespeare, The Merchant of Venice *(1596-8)* II.ii •692

Honour thy father and thy mother.

Bible, Exodus 20.12 •693

I prithee, daughter, do not make me mad.

William Shakespeare, King Lear *(1605-6)* II.iv •694

A slavish bondage to parents cramps every faculty of the mind.

Mary Wollstonecraft, A Vindication of the Rights of Woman, *(1792)* •696

An unhappy alternative is before you, Elizabeth. From this day you must be a stranger to one of your parents. Your mother will never see you again if you do not marry Mr Collins, and I will never see you again if you do.

Mr Bennet's finest moment, in Jane Austen's Pride and Prejudice *(1813)* •695

A wise son maketh a glad father: but a foolish son is the heaviness of his mother. Bible, Proverbs 10.1 •697

He that spareth his rod hateth his son
Bible, Proverbs 13.24 •698

Man hands on
  misery to man.

It deepens like a
  coastal shelf.

Get out as early
  as you can,

And don't have
  any kids yourself.

Philip Larkin, 'This Be the Verse' *1974* •699

Girls scream,
Boys shout;
Dogs bark,
School's out.

W.H. Davies, 'School's Out'; *published in* Collected Poems *(1963)* •700

The direction in which education starts a man will determine his future life. *Plato* •701

Education ent only books and music — it's asking questions, all the time.

Arnold Wesker, Roots *1959* •702

Knowledge which is acquired under compulsion has no hold on the mind. Therefore do not use compulsion, but let early education be rather a sort of amusement. This will better enable you to find out the natural bent of the child.

Plato, with a sentiment shared by schoolchildren everywhere. •703

The roots of education are bitter, but the fruit is sweet.

Aristotle, in **Diogenes Laertius, Lives of Philosophers** •704

It is no matter what you teach them [children] first, any more than what leg you shall put into your breeches first.

Samuel Johnson, in **Boswell's Life of Samuel Johnson** *(1791) 26 July 1763* •705

EDUCATION. — At Mr Wackford Squeer's Academy, Dotheboys Hall, at the delightful village of Dotheboys, near Greta Bridge in Yorkshire, Youth are boarded, clothed, booked, furnished with pocket-money, provided with all necessaries, instructed in all languages, living and dead, mathematics, orthography, geometry, trigonometry, the use of the globes, algebra, single stick (if required), writing, arithmetic, fortification, and every other branch of classical literature. Terms, twenty guineas per annum. No extras, no vacations, and diet unparalleled.

Charles Dickens, **Nicholas Nickleby** *(1839)* •706

We class schools, you see, into four grades: Leading school, First-rate School, Good school, and School. Frankly,' said Mr Levy, 'School is pretty bad.'

Evelyn Waugh, **Decline and Fall** *(1928)* •707

C-l-e-a-n, clean, verb active, to make bright, to scour. W-i-n, win, d-e-r, der, winder, a casement. When a boy knows this out of the book, he goes and does it.

Charles Dickens, Nicholas Nickleby *(1839)* •708

Ignorance is like a delicate exotic fruit; touch it and the bloom is gone. The whole theory of modern education is radically unsound. Fortunately, in England, at any rate, education produces no effect whatsoever.

Oscar Wilde, The Importance of Being Earnest *(1895)* •709

'I don't care a straw for Greek particle, or the digamma, no more does his mother. What is he sent to school for?… If he'll only turn out a brave, helpful, truth-telling Englishman, and a gentleman, and a Christian, that's all I want,' thought the Squire.

Thomas Hughes, Thomas Brown's Schooldays *(1857)* •710

I pay the schoolmaster, but 'tis the schoolboys that educate my son.

Ralph Waldo Emerson, Journals •711

For every person who wants to teach there are approximately thirty who don't want to learn — much.

W.C. Sellar and R.J. Yeatman, And Now All This *(1932)* •712

It is when the gods hate a man with uncommon abhorrence that they drive him into the profession of a schoolmaster.

Seneca, Epistolae and Lucilium, *AD 64* •713

'That's the reason they're called lessons,' the Gryphon remarked: 'because they lessen from day to day.' *Lewis Carroll,* **Alice's Adventures in Wonderland** *(1865)* •714

Multiplication is vexation,
Division is as bad;
The Rule of Three doth
  puzzle me,
And Practice drives me mad.
Anonymous, **Lean's Collectanea vol.4**
(1904); possibly 16th-century •715

The only good things about skool are the BOYS WIZZ who are noble brave fearless etc. although you hav various swots, bulies, cissies, milksops, greedy guts and oiks with whom I am forced to mingle hem-hem.
Geoffrey Willans and Ronald Searle, **Down With Skool!** *(1953)* •716

Alas, regardless of their doom,
The little victims play!
No sense have they of ills to come,
Nor care beyond a day
Thomas Gray, 'Ode on a Distant Prospect of Eton College' *(1747)* •717

The scholar who cherishes the love of comfort, is not fit to be deemed a scholar.

Confucius, **Analects** •718

There is now less flogging in our great schools than formerly, but then less is learned there; so what the boys get at one end they lose at the other.
Samuel Johnson, in James Boswell, **Life of Samuel Johnson** *(1791) 1775* •719

The dread of beatings!
Dread of being late!

And, greatest dread of all,
the dread of games!

John Betjeman,
'Summoned by Bells' *(1960)* •720

Public schools are
the nurseries of all
vice and immorality.

Henry Fielding, Joseph Andrews *(1742)* •722

He must have known me
had he seen me as he was
wont to see me, for he was
in the habit of flogging
me constantly. Perhaps
he did not recognize
me by my face.

Anthony Trollope, of his headmaster,
Autobiography *(1883)* •721

Good gracious, you've
got to educate him first.
You can't expect a boy
to be vicious till he's
been to a good school.

Saki, Reginald in Russia *(1910)* •723

Dost thou think, because thou art virtuous, that there shall be no more cakes and ale?

William Shakespeare,
Twelfth Night *(1601)* II.iii •724

It is better to waste one's youth than to do nothing with it at all.

Georges Courteline, French dramatist and novelist, La Philosophie de Georges Courteline *(1948)* •725

I would there were no age between ten and three-and-twenty, or that youth would sleep out the rest; for there is nothing in the between but getting wenches with child, wronging the ancientry, stealing, fighting.

William Shakespeare,
The Winter's Tale III.iii •726

The young always have the same problem — how to rebel and conform at the same time. They have now solved this by defying their parents and copying one another.

Quentin Crisp,
The Naked Civil Servant. •727

Undergraduates owe their chief happiness to the consciousness that they are no longer at school. The nonsense which was knocked out of them at school is all put gently back into them at Oxford or Cambridge. *Max Beerbohm,* More *(1899)* •728

The exquisite art of idleness, one of the most important things that any university can teach.

Oscar Wilde •729

Let schoolmasters puzzle their brain,

With grammar, and nonsense, and learning,

Good liquor, I stoutly maintain,

Gives genius a better discerning.

Oliver Goldsmith, She Stoops to Conquer *(1773)* •730

It was remarked to me… that to play billiards well was a sign of an ill-spent youth.

English philosopher and journalist Herbert Spencer, in Duncan, Life and Letters of Spencer *(1908)* •731

If I had no duties, and no reference to futurity, I would spend my life in driving briskly in a post-chaise with a pretty woman.

Samuel Johnson, in Boswell, Life of Samuel Johnson *(1791), 19 September 1777* •732

Cheerfulness gives elasticity to the spirit. Spectres fly before it.
Samuel Smiles, **Self-Help** *(1859)* •733

It would be mortifying to the feelings of many ladies, could they be made to understand how little the heart of man is affected by what is costly or new in their attire.
Jane Austen, **Northanger Abbey** *(1818)* •734

Live all you can; it's a mistake not to. It doesn't so much matter what you do in particular, so long as you have your life. If you haven't had that, what have you had? *Henry James,* **The Ambassadors** *(1903)* •735

One cannot have too large a party. A large party secures its own amusement. *Jane Austen,* **Emma** *(1816)* •736

All the adaptations I saw before were with people in stiff suits standing up very straight making polite conversation through pursed lips in drawing rooms. But I felt the story is more about young men and women in the prime of their lives with lots of hormones pounding around.
Andrew Davies on **Pride and Prejudice,** *which he adapted for the BBC. Speaking at Banff Television Festival 1999* •737

A merry heart doeth good like a medicine.

Bible, Proverbs 17:22 •738

A man hath no better thing under the sun, than to eat, and to drink, and to be merry.

Bible, Ecclessiastes 8:15 •739

A cigarette is the perfect type of a perfect pleasure. It is exquisite and leaves one quite unsatisfied. What more can one want?

Oscar Wilde •740

The road of excess leads to the palace of wisdom.

William Blake, The Marriage of Heaven and Hell *(1790-93)* •741

LSD? Nothing much happened, but I did get the distinct impression that some birds were trying to communicate with me.

W.H. Auden, in George Plimpton (ed.), The Writer's Chapbook *(1989)* •742

149

Man, being reasonable, must get drunk;
The best of life is but intoxication.
Lord Byron, **Don Juan** *(1819-24)* •743

What does drunkenness not
accomplish? It unlocks
secrets, confirms our hopes,
urges the indolent into battle,
lifts the burden from anxious
minds, teaches new arts.
Horace •744

And malt does more than Milton can
To justify God's ways to man.
Ale, man, ale's the stuff to drink
For fellows whom it hurts to think.
A.E. Housman, **A Shropshire Lad** *(1896)* •745

Gin-and-water is the source of all my inspiration.
Lord Byron, **Conversations** *(1824)* •746

We'll drink one another's healths, and spoil our own.
Jerome K. Jerome, **Idle Thoughts of an Idle Fellow** *(1889)* •747

Wine leads to folly. It makes even the wisest laugh too much. It makes him dance. It makes him say what should have been left unsaid.

Homer •748

Breslin's Rule: Don't trust a brilliant idea unless it survives a hangover.

Jimmy Breslin •749

Let us have wine and women, mirth and laughter,
Sermons and soda-water the day after.

Lord Byron, **Don Juan** *(1819-24)* •750

After the first glass of absinthe, you see things as you wish they were. After the second, you see them as they are not. Finally, you see things as they really are and that is the most horrible thing in the world.

Oscar Wilde •751

I remember my youth and the feeling that will never come back any more — the feeling that I could last forever, outlast the sea, the earth, and all men

Joseph Conrad, **Youth** •752

My salad days,
When I was green in judgement.

William Shakespeare,
Anthony and Cleopatra *(1606-7)* I.v •753

To find a young fellow that is
neither a wit in his own eye,
nor a fool in the eye of the world,
is a very hard task.

William Congreve, **Love for Love** *(1695)* •754

Of all the horrid, hideous
notes of woe,

Sadder than owl-songs
or the midnight blast,

Is that portentous phrase,
'I told you so'.

Lord Byron, **Don Juan** *(1819-24)* •755

The devil's most devilish
when respectable.

Elizabeth Barrett Browning,
Aurora Leigh *(1857)* •756

At twenty years of age,
the will reigns; at thirty,
the wit; and at forty,
the judgement.

Benjamin Franklin, **Poor
Richard's Almanac** *(1741)* •758

Nel mezzo del
cammin di nostra
vita. — Midway
along the path
of our life.

Dante Alighieri 1265-1321,
Divina Commedia, 'Inferno' •757

…when I became
a man I put away
childish things.

Bible, I Corinthians 13.1 •759

When I was ten, I read fairy tales in secret, and would have been ashamed of being found doing so. Now that I am fifty, I read them openly. When I became a man, I put away childish things, including the fear of childishness and the desire to be very grown up.

C.S. Lewis, 'On Three Ways of Writing for Children' *(1952)* •760

Be wise with speed;
A fool at forty is a fool indeed.
Edward Young, 'The Love of Fame' *(1725-8)* •761

One of the pleasures of middle age is to find out that one WAS right, and that one was much righter than one knew at say 17 or 23.

Ezra Pound, ABC of Reading *(1934)* •762

There is no good end attained by trying to persuade ourselves that women are all incorporeal, angelic, colourless, passionless, helpless creatures...Women have especial need, as the world goes, to be shrewd, self-reliant, and strong; and we do all we can in our literature to render them helpless, imbecile, and idiotic.

Justin McCarthy, in Westminster Review *1864* •763

It is no use telling me that there are bad aunts and good aunts. At the core they are all alike. Sooner or later, out pops the cloven hoof.

P.G. Wodehouse, The Code of the Woosters •764

Mrs Badcock and two young women were of the same party, except when Mrs Badcock thought herself obliged to leave them to run around the room after her drunken husband. His avoidance, and her pursuit, with the probable intoxication of both, was an amusing scene.

Jane Austen, **Letter to her sister, Cassandra** •765

All happy families resemble one another, but each unhappy family is unhappy in its own way.

Leo Tolstoy, **Anna Karenina** *(1875-77)* •766

Good breeding consists in concealing how much we think of ourselves and how little we think of other persons.

Mark Twain, **Notebook,** *1935* •767

Every idiot who goes about with Merry Christmas on his lips should be boiled with his own pudding, and buried with a stake of holly through his heart.

Charles Dickens, **A Christmas Carol** *(1843)* •768

A servant's too often a negligent elf;
— If it's business of consequence,
DO IT YOURSELF!

R. H. Barham, 'The Ingoldsby Penence!
— **Moral'** *(1842)* •769

You think that I am cruel and gluttonous when I beat my cook for sending in a bad dinner. But if that is too trivial a cause, what other can there be for beating a cook? *Martial* •770

More childish valorous than manly wise.

Christopher Marlowe,
Tamburlaine the Great *(1590)* •771

To his dog, every man is Napoleon; hence the constant popularity of dogs.

Aldous Huxley •772

The proper office of a friend is to side with you when you are in the wrong. Nearly anybody will side with you when you are in the right.

Mark Twain, **Notebooks,** *1935* •773

It's no good trying to keep up old friendships. It's painful for both sides. The fact is, one grows out of people, and the only thing is to face it.

Novelist and short-story writer
W. Somerset Maugham,
Cakes and Ale, *1930.* •774

The heart may think it knows better: the senses know absence blots people out. We have really no absent friends.

Anglo-Irish novelist and short-story writer Elizabeth Bowen, Death of the Heart, *1938* •775

It is better to be beautiful than to be good. But… it is better to be good than to be ugly.

Oscar Wilde, The Picture of Dorian Gray *(1891)* •776

The flowers anew, returning
  seasons bring;
But beauty faded has no
  second spring.

Ambrose Philips, The First Pastoral *(1708)* •777

I am resolved to grow fat
and look young till forty,
and then slip out of the world
with the first wrinkle and the
reputation of five-and-twenty.

John Dryden, The Maiden Queen *(1668)* •778

Rough winds do shake the darling
  buds of May,
And summer's lease hath all too
  short a date.

William Shakespeare,
Sonnet 18 •779

157

We have followed too much the devices and desires of our own hearts.

The Book of Common Prayer *(1662),* **Morning Prayer General Confession** •780

I don't like baths, I don't enjoy them in the slightest and, if I could, I'd prefer to go around dirty.

J.B. Priestley, The Observer, *1979* •782

Up, and at my chamber all morning in the office, doing business and also reading a little of L'École des Filles, which is a mighty lewd book, but yet not amiss for a sober man once read over to inform himself in the villainy of the world.

Samuel Pepys, Diary *1668. Sober man indeed — that's what they all say* •781

The truth is, that in London it is always a sickly season. Nobody is healthy in London, nobody can be.

Jane Austen, Mr Woodhouse in Emma *(1816)* •783

My life is one demd horrid grind!

Charles Dickens, Nicholas Nickleby *(1839)* •784

Success is relative:
It is what we can make of the
    mess we have made of things.

T.S. Eliot, **The Family Reunion** *(1939)* •787

I refuse to endure months of
expensive humiliation only to be
told that at the age of four I was
in love with my rocking-horse.

Noël Coward on 'therapy' •785

Every man has a lurking wish to appear considerable in his native place.

Samuel Johnson, letter to Joshua Reynolds,
17 July 1771 •788

He was meddling too much in my private life.

Tennessee Williams on why he had given up visiting his psychoanalyst •786

If you would not be forgotten
as soon as you are dead, either
write things worth reading or
do things worth writing.

US statesman Benjamin Franklin,
attrib. •789

159

They are not long, the days
  of wine and roses:

Out of a misty dream

Our path emerges for a while,
  then closes

Within a dream.

> *Ernest Dowson,*
> **'Vitae Summa Brevis'** *(1896)* •790

We wove a web in childhood,
A web of sunny air;
We dug a spring in infancy
Of water pure and fair;
We sowed in youth a mustard seed,
We cut an almond rod;
We are now grown to riper age —
Are they withered in the sod?

> *Charlotte Brontë,*
> **'We wove a web in childhood'**
> *(written 1835)* •791

As they say, when the
age is in, the wit is out.

William Shakepeare, **Much Ado
About Nothing III.v** *(1598)* •792

I have a bone to pick with Fate,
Come here and tell me, girlie,
Do you think my mind is
  maturing late,
Or simply rotted early?

Ogden Nash, 'Lines on Facing Forty' *(1942)* •793

No arts; no letters; no society;
and which is worst of all,
continual fear and danger
of violent death; and the life
of man, solitary, poor, nasty,
brutish, and short.

> *Thomas Hobbes,*
> **Leviathan** *(1651)* •794

But at my back I always hear
Time's wingèd chariot hurrying near:
And yonder all before us lie
Deserts of vast eternity.

Andrew Marvell, 'To His Coy Mistress' *(1681)*
•795

At thirty a man suspects
   himself a fool;

Knows it at forty, and reforms
   his plan;

at Fifty chides his infamous
   delay,

Pushes his prudent purpose
   to resolve;

In all the magnaminity
   of thought

Resolves; and re-resolves;
   then dies the same.

Edward Young, Night Thoughts *(1742-45)* •796

We had the experience but missed the meaning.

T.S. Eliot, Four Quartets,
'The Dry Salvages' *(1941)* •797

161

Do not go gentle in to that good night,
Old age should burn and rave at close
of day; Rage, rage against the dying
of the light.

Dylan Thomas, **'Do Not Go Gentle into
that Good Night'** *(1952)* •798

No one is so old that he does not think he could live another year.

Roman orator and statesman Cicero,
De Senectute, *44 BC.* •800

I grow old… I grow old…
I shall wear the bottoms of
my trousers rolled.

T.S. Eliot, **'The Love Song of
J. Alfred Prufrock'** *(1917)* •799

Gather ye rosebuds while ye may,
Old Time is still a-flying; and this same
flower that smiles today
tomorrow will be dying.
Robert Herrick, *(1591-1674)* •801

Is not old wine wholesomest,
old pippins toothsomest,
old wood burn brightest,
old linen wash whitest?
Old soldiers, sweethearts,
are surest, and old lovers
are soundest.

> *John Webster,*
> **Westward Ho!** *(1607)* •802

Age does not make us childish,
as men tell

It merely finds us children
still at heart.

> *Johann Wolfgang von Goethe,*
> **Faust pt.1** *(1808)* •803

It is better to be seventy years
young than forty years old!

*Oliver Wendell Holmes, in reply to an
invitation from Julia Ward Howe to her
seventieth birthday party, 27 May 1889* •804

We talked about growing
old gracefully

And Elsie, who's seventy-four,

Said, 'A, it's a question of being
sincere, and

B, if you're supple you've
nothing to fear.'

Then she swung upside down
from a glass chandelier.

I couldn't have liked it more.

Noël Coward, **I've been to a Marvellous
Party'.** *Set to music, 1938* •805

Though I look old, I am strong and lusty

William Shakespeare, **As You Like It** *(1599)* •806

163

No spring, nor summer
beauty hath such grace,
as I have seen in one
autumnal face.

Poet and divine John Donne,
'The Autumnal', Elegy 9, *(1634)* •807

No pleasure is worth giving
up for the sake of two more
years in a geriatric home in
Weston-super-Mare.

Kingsley Amis, in The Times
21 June 1994 (attrib.) •808

Grow old along with me!
The best is yet to be.

Robert Browning,
'Rabbi Ben Ezra' *(1864)*
•809

How happy he who crowns in
shades like these,

A youth of labour with an
age of ease.

Oliver Goldsmith, The Deserted Village *(1770)*
•810

As you are old
and reverend, you
should be wise.

William Shakespeare, King Lear *(1605-06)*
I.iv •811

The oldest hath borne most:
we that are young, shall never
see so much, nor live so long.

William Shakespeare, King Lear *(1605-6)* V.iii
•812

From the earliest times the old have rubbed it into the young that they are wiser than they, and before the young had discovered what nonsense this was they were old too, and it profited them to carry on the imposture. *W. Somerset Maugham,* **Cakes and Ale** *(1930)* •813

W'en folks git ole en strucken wid de palsy, dey mus speck ter be laff'd at.

Joel Chandler Harris, **Nights with Uncle Remus** *(1883)* •814

Age is deformed, youth unkind,
We scorn their bodies, they our mind.
Thomas Bastard, **Chrestoleros** *(1598)* •815

All that I have said and done,
Now that I am old and ill,
Turns into a question till
I lie awake night after night
And never get the answers right.
W.B. Yeats, 'The Man and the Echo' *(1939)* •816

See how old age its
  veterans rewards!
A youth of frolics,
  an old age of cards.
Alexander Pope, **Epistles to Several Persons** 'To a Lady' *(1735)* •817

When you are old and
  grey and full of sleep,

And nodding by the fire,
  take down this book

And slowly read and
  dream of the soft look

Your eyes had once, and
  of their shadows deep.

W.B. Yeats, 'When You Are Old' *(1893)*
•818

What are those blue
  remembered hills,

What spires, what
  farms are those?

That is the land of
  lost content,

I see it shining plain,

The happy highways
  where I went

And cannot
  come again.

A.E. Housman, A Shropshire Lad *(1896)* •819

I have had playmates,
  I have had companions,

In my days of childhood, in
  my joyful school-days —

All, all are gone, the
  old familiar faces.

  Charles Lamb 1775-1834,
  'The Old Familiar Faces' •820

How often are we to die before
we go quite off this stage? In
every friend we lose a part of
ourselves, and the best part.

Alexander Pope, **letter to Jonathan Swift,**
5 December 1732 •821

Senescence begins and
  middle age ends

The day your descendants
  outnumber your friends.

Ogden Nash, **'Crossing the Border',**
You Can't Get There from Here, *(1957)* •822

And so, from hour to hour,
  we ripe and ripe,

And then, from hour to hour,
  we rot and rot:

And thereby hangs a tale.

William Shakespeare,
As You Like It *(1599)* II.vii •825

Even such is time, which takes in trust
Our youth, our joys, and all we have,
And pays us but with age and dust.

*Walter Raleigh, written the night before
his death in 1618* •823

The days of our age are threescore
years and ten; and though men be
so strong that they come to fourscore
years, yet is their strength then but
labour and sorrow; so soon passeth
it away, and we are gone.

Bible, Psalm 90 •826

Every man desires to live long; but no man would be old.

Jonathan Swift, **Thoughts on
Various Subjects** *(1727 ed.)* •824

I wasted time, and now doth time waste me.

William Shakespeare, **Richard II** *(1595)* V.v •827

Though nothing can bring
  back the hour
Of splendour in the grass,
  of glory in the flower;
We will grieve not,
  rather find
Strength in what
  remains behind.
In the faith that looks
  through death,
In years that bring the
  philosophic mind.

William Wordsworth, 'Ode.
Intimations of Immortality' *(1807)* •828

And almost every one when age,
Disease, or sorrows strike him,
Inclines to think there is a God,
Or something very like Him.

Arthur Hugh Clough, 'Dipsychus' *(1865)* •829

For when the One Great Scorer

 comes to mark against your name,

He marks — not that you won or lost

 — but how you played the Game.

US writer Grantland Rice,
'Alumnus Football' *(1941)* •830

Oh, what a dear ravishing thing
is the beginning of an Amour!

Aphra Behn, The Emperor of the Moon *(1687)* •831

Love sought is good,
but giv'n unsought
is better.

William Shakespeare,
Twelfth Night *(1601)* III.i •834

In the spring a young man's
fancy lightly turns
to thoughts of love.

Alfred, Lord Tennyson,
'Locksley Hall' *(1842)* •832

Love is the irresistible
desire to be irresistibly
desired. *Robert Frost* •835

O! How this spring of love resembleth
The uncertain glory of an April day.

William Shakespeare,
Two Gentlemen of Verona
(1592-3) I.iii •833

Drink to me only with thine
eyes, and I will pledge with mine,
or leave a kiss upon the cup,
and I'll not look for wine.

Playwright and poet Ben Jonson,
'To Celia', *1616* •836

Love is the wisdom of the fool and the folly of the wise.

Samuel Johnson, in William Cooke, Life of Samuel Foote *(1805)* •837

The lunatic, the lover, and the poet,
Are of imagination all compact.

William Shakespeare, A Midummer Night's Dream *(1595-6)* V.i •838

My love for Linton is like the foliage in the woods; time will change it, I'm well aware, as winter changes the trees — My love for Heathcliff resembles the eternal rocks beneath: — a source of little visible delight, but necessary.   *Emily Brontë,* Wuthering Heights *(1847)* •839

I will be horribly in love with her.
Benedick of the equally scornful Beatrice, in William Shakespeare's Much Ado About Nothing II.iii *(1598)* •840

The heart has its reasons which reason knows nothing of.

Blaise Pascal, Pensees *(1670)* •841

The speaking in perpetual hyperbole is comely in nothing but in love

Francis Bacon, Essays *(1625)* 'Of Love' •842

O wonderful, wonderful, and
most wonderful wonderful!
And yet again wonderful, and
after that, out of all whooping!

William Shakespeare, **As You Like It**
(1599) III.ii •843

Can he wel speke of love? quod she

Geoffrey Chaucer, **Troilus and Criseyde,**
Book II •844

All a lovers' wish can reach
For the joy my love shall teach
And for thy Pleasure shall improve
All that Art can add to love.
Yet still I love thee without Art,
Ancient person of my heart.

Courtier and poet John Wilmot,
Earl of Rochester, 'A Song of a
Young Lady to her Ancient Lover' •845

I'll love you, dear, I'll love you
Till China and Africa meet
And the river jumps over the mountain
And the salmon sing in the street,
I'll love you till the ocean
Is folded and hung up to dry
And the seven stars go squawking
Like geese about the sky.

W.H. Auden, 'As I Walked
Out One Evening' *(1940)* •846

And she was as fayr as is the rose in May.

Geoffrey Chaucer, **The Legend of Good**
Women, 'Cleopatra' •847

O, she doth teach the torches to burn bright!

William Shakespeare, Romeo and Juliet, *(1595)* I.v •848

O, my Luve's like a red, red rose
That's newly sprung in June;
O my Luve's like the melodie
That's sweetly play'd in tune.

Robert Burns, 'A Red Red Rose' *(1796), derived from various folk songs* •849

She knows her man, and
  when you rant and swear,
Can draw you to her
  with a single hair.

John Dryden, translation of Persius Satires •850

Pains of love be sweeter far
than all other pleasures are.

Poet and playwright John Dryden, Tyrannic Love, *1669* •851

Love is not love
Which alters when it alteration finds.

William Shakespeare, Sonnet 116 •852

My true love hath my heart
  and I have his,
By just exchange one for
  the other giv'n;
I hold his dear, and mine
  he cannot miss,
There never was a better
  bargain driv'n.

Philip Sidney, Arcadia *(1581)* •853

To love is to admire
with the heart; to admire
is to love with the mind.

French man of letters Theophile Gautier •854

What I have done is yours;
what I have to do is yours;
being part in all I have,
devoted yours.

William Shakespeare,
The Rape of Lucrece *(1595)* •856

How do I love thee?
Let me count the
ways. I love thee
to the depth and
breadth and height
My soul can reach.

Poet Elizabeth Barrett Browning
'Sonnets from the Portuguese'.
No. 43, *1850* •855

To say a man is fallen in love, — or
that he is deeply in love, — or up to
the ears in love, — and sometimes
even head over heels in it, — carries
an idiomatical kind of implication,
that love is a thing below a man.

Laurence Sterne,
Tristram Shandy *1759-67*
•857

Love has no
other desire but
to fulfil itself.

Syrian writer and artist Kahlil Gibran,
The Prophet, *1923* •858

What is love? 'tis not hereafter;
Present mirth hath present laughter;
What's to come is still unsure:
In delay there lies no plenty;
Then come kiss me, sweet and twenty,
Youth's a stuff will not endure.
William Shakespeare, Twelfth Night, II. ii
(1601) •859

Where do the noses go?
I always wondered where
the noses would go.
Ernest Hemingway, For Whom
the Bell Tolls *(1940)* •860

This wondrous miracle
did Love devise,
For dancing is love's
proper exercise.
John Davies, 'Orchestra,
or a Poem of Dancing' *(1596)* •861

All the privilege I claim for
my own sex... is that of loving
longest, when existence or
when hope is gone.
Jane Austen, Persuasion, *(1818)* •862

One word frees us
from all the weight
and pain of life.
That word is love.
Sophocles •863

Give me my Romeo; and, when he
shall die, take him and cut him out in
little stars, and he will make the face
of heaven so fine that all the world
will be in love with night and pay
no worship to the garish sun.
William Shakespeare,
Romeo and Juliet, *(1595)* III.ii •864

The magic of first love is our ignorance that it can ever end.

Benjamin Disraeli, Henrietta Temple *(1837)*
•865

I wish you could invent some means to make me at all happy without you. Every hour I am more and more concentrated in you; everything else tastes like chaff in my mouth.
John Keats, letter to Fanny Brawne,
August 1820 •866

I hold it true, whate'er befall; I feel it, when I sorrow most; 'Tis better to have loved and lost than never to have loved at all.

Poet Lord Tennyson,
In Memoriam A.H.H., *(1850),*
Canto 28 •867

He was my North,
 my South, my East,
 my West,
My working week
 and my Sunday rest,
My noon, my midnight,
 my talk, my song;
I thought that love
 would last for ever.
I was wrong.

W.H. Auden, '**Funeral Blues**',
originally in the play
The Ascent of F6 *1937* •868

Though they go mad they
 shall be sane,
Though they sink through the
 sea they shall rise again;
Though lovers be lost,
 love shall not;
And death shall have
 no dominion.

Welsh poet and writer Dylan Thomas,
'**And Death Shall Have No Dominion**', *1936*
•869

Take away love and
our earth is a tomb.

Poet Robert Browning •870

Omnia vincit Amor: et nos cedamus
Amori. — Love conquers all things:
let us too give in to Love.

Virgil, Eclogues •871

She was the beat of my
heart for thirty years.
She was the music heard
faintly on the edge of sound.
It was my great and now
useless regret that I never
wrote anything really worth
her attention, no book that
I could dedicate to her.
I planned it. I thought of it,
but I never wrote it. Perhaps
I couldn't have written it.

*Raymond Chandler after the death
of his wife,* **letter to Leonard Russell,**
29 December 1954 •872

Reader, I married him.

Charlotte Brontë, **Jane Eyre** *(1847)* •873

Flesh of Flesh,

Bone of my One thou art,
  and from thy State,

Mine shall never be
  parted, weal or woe.

John Milton, **Paradise Lost** *(1667)* •874

Marriage is the greatest
earthly happiness when
founded on complete
sympathy. *Benjamin Disraeli,*
letter to Gladstone •875

I sing of brooks, of blossoms, birds, and bowers:

Of April, May, of June and July-flowers.

I sing of May-poles, wassails, wakes,

Of bride-grooms, brides, and of their bridal-cakes.

Robert Herrick, 'The Argument of
his Book' from Hesperides *(1648)* •876

The joys of marriage are
  the heaven on earth,
Life's paradise, great princess,
  the soul's quiet.
John Ford, The Broken Heart *(1633)* II.ii •877

Love seems the swiftest but it is
the slowest of all growths. No man
or woman really knows what a
perfect love is until they have been
married a quarter of a century.
Mark Twain, Notebook *1894* •878

People talk about beautiful friendships between
two persons of the same sex. What is the best
of that sort, as compared with the friendship
of man and wife, where the best impulses and
highest ideals of both are the same? There is
no place for comparison between the two
friendships; the one is earthly, the other divine.
Mark Twain, A Connecticut Yankee *(1889)*
•879

What a happy and holy fashion it is that
those who love one another should rest
on the same pillow.
Nathaniel Hawthorne •880

Opening her eyes again,
and seeing her husband's
face across the table,
she leaned forward to
give it a pat on the cheek,
and sat down to supper,
declaring it to be the
best face in the world.
Charles Dickens, Our Mutual Friend *(1865)* •881

The quiet mutual gaze of a trusting husband and wife is like the first moment of rest or refuge from a great weariness or a great danger.

George Eliot, Silas Marner *(1861)* •882

She is a woman, therefore may be wooed;
She is a woman, therefore may be won.

William Shakespeare,
Titus Andronicus *(1590)* II.i •884

A lady's imagination is very rapid; it jumps from admiration to love, from love to matrimony in a moment. *Jane Austen, Mr Darcy in* Pride and Prejudice *(1813)*
•885

And at home by the fire, whenever you look up, there I shall be — and whenever I look up there you will be.

Thomas Hardy, Far from the Madding Crowd *(1874). Gabriel Oak proposing to Bathsheba Everdene.* •883

I never had one hour's happiness in her society, and yet my mind all round the four-and-twenty hours was harping on the happiness of having her with me unto death. *Charles Dickens,*
Great Expectations *(1861)*
•886

183

Mr Richard Harvey is going to be married; but as it is a great secret and only known to half the neighbourhood, you must not mention it.

Jane Austen, Letter to her sister, Cassandra •887

Miranda: My husband then?
Ferdinand: Ay, with a heart as willing
As bondage e'er of freedom.

William Shakespeare,
The Tempest *(1611)* III.i •888

'My lige lady, generally,' quod he,
'Wommen desiren to have
   sovereynetee
As wel over hir housbond as
   hir love'.

Geoffrey Chaucer, The Canterbury Tales, 'Wife of Bath's Tale' •889

Being a husband is a whole-time job. That is why so many husbands fail at it. They cannot give their entire attention to it.

Arnold Bennett, The Title *(1918)* Act 1 •890

If you are afraid of loneliness, don't marry.

Anton Chekhov •891

184

Marriage has many pains, but celibacy has no pleasures.

Samuel Johnson, **Rasselas,** *(1759)* •892

You shall be together when the white wings of death scatter your days. Ay, you shall be together even in the silent memory of God. But let there be spaces in your togetherness, and let the winds of the heavens dance between you.

Syrian writer and artist Kahlil Gibran, 'On Marriage', in **The Prophet,** *(1923)* •893

The sum which two married people owe to one another defies calculation. It is an infinite debt, which can only be discharged through eternity.

Johnann Wolfgang von Goethe •894

Of soup and love,
the first is the best.

Thomas Fuller, **Gnomologia** *(1732)* •895

In her first passion
woman loves her lover,
in all the others all she
loves is love.

Lord Byron, **Don Juan**, *1819-24* •897

Ay me! for aught that ever
  I could read,

could ever hear by tale
  or history,

the course of true love never
  did run smooth.

William Shakespeare, **A Midsummer
Night's Dream**, *(1595-6)* I.i •896

A good uniform must
work its way with the
women, sooner or later.

Charles Dickens, **Pickwick Papers** *(1837)* •898

My only books
Were woman's looks,
And folly's all they've taught me

Thomas Moore, 'The time I've
lost in wooing' *1807* •899

Judgement of beauty can err, what with the wine and the dark.

Ovid •900

Keep you in the rear of your affection,
Out of the shot and danger of desire.

William Shakespeare, Hamlet *(1601)* I.iii
— Laertes advises his sister Ophelia •901

Affection is a coal that
  must be cool'd;
Else, sufer'd, it will set
  the heart on fire.

> *William Shakespeare,*
> Venus and Adonis,*(1593)*
> stanza 65 •902

Someone asked Sophocles, 'How is your sex-life now? Are you still able to have a woman?' He replied, 'Hush, man; most gladly am I rid of it all, as though I had escaped from a mad and savage master.'

Sophocles (in Plato's Republic) •903

Love is just a dirty trick on us to achieve the continuation of the species.

W. Somerset Maugham,
A Writers Notebook, *1949* •904

Love built on beauty, soon as beauty, dies.

John Donne, Elegies 'The Anagram' *(c.1595)*
•905

187

No one would ever have fallen in love unless he had first read about it.

Duc de la Rochefoucauld, in Edmund White, The Burning Library *(1994)*; attrib. •906

I have met women whom I really think would like to be married to a poem and to be given away by a novel.

John Keats, letter to Fanny Brawne, *8 July 1819* •907

Love is a grave mental disease.
Plato •908

My heart is a lonely hunter that hunts on a lonely hill.
Fiona McLeod, 'The Lonely Hunter' *(1896)* •909

Love is like any other luxury. You have no right to it unless you can afford it.

Anthony Trollope, The Way We Live Now *(1875)* •910

It is a truth universally acknowledged, that a single man in possession of a good fortune, must be in want of a wife.

Jane Austen, **Pride and Prejudice** •911

Love and a cottage! Eh, Fanny! Ah, give me indifference and a coach and six!

George Colman, the Elder, and David Garrick, The Clandestine Marriage *(1766)* •913

It would be an excellent match, for he was rich, and she was handsome.

Jane Austen, **Sense and Sensibility** *(1811)* •912

Oh, life is a glorious cycle of song,

A medley of extemporanea;

And love is a thing that can never go wrong;

And I am Marie of Roumania.

Dorothy Parker, 'Comment' *(1937)* •914

It was a blonde.
A blonde to make
a bishop kick a hole in
a stained glass window.

American detective fiction writer Raymond Chandler, Farewell My Lovely, *(1940)* •915

Personal beauty is a greater recommendation than any letter of reference.

Aristotle •916

And what is bettre than wisedoom?
Womman. And what is bettre than
a good womman? Nothyng.

Chaucer, The Canterbury Tales, 'The Tale of Melibee' •917

Ful smale ypulled were hire browes two,
And tho were bent and blake as any sloo. —
(She'd thinned out carefully her eyebrows two,
And they were arched and black as any sloe)

Geoffrey Chaucer, The Canterbury Tales, 'The Miller's Tale' •918

That's the thing about girls.
Every time they do something
pretty, even if they're not much
to look at, or even if they're sort
of stupid, you fall half in love
with them and then you never
know where the hell you are.
Girls. Jesus Christ. They can
drive you crazy, they really can.

J.D. Salinger, The Catcher in the Rye, *(1951)* •919

Tisn't beauty, so to speak,
nor good talk necessarily.
It's just It. Some women'll
stay in a man's memory if they
once walked down a street.
Rudyard Kipling, Travels and
Discoveries *(1904)* •920

She just wore
Enough for modesty — no more.
Robert Buchanan 'White Rose and Red'
(1873) •921

It is very often nothing
but our own vanity that
deceives us. Women fancy
admiration means more
than it does. *Jane Austen,*
Jane Bennet in
Pride and Prejudice
(1813) •922

Chastity — the most
unnatural of all sexual
perversions. *Aldous Huxley,*
Eyeless in Gaza
(1936) •923

Sexual intercourse began
In nineteen sixty-three
(Which was rather late for me) —
Between the end of the Chatterley ban
And the Beatles' first LP.
Philip Larkin, 'Annus Mirabilis' *(1974)* •924

He who desires but acts
not, breeds pestilence.
William Blake, The Marriage of Heaven
and Hell *(1790-93)* •925

She knew how to allure by denying,
and to make the gift rich by delaying it.
Anthony Trollope, Phineas Finn *(1869)* •926

191

Licence my roving hands,
  and let them go,
Behind, before, above,
  between, below.
O my America, my new
  found land,
My kingdom, safeliest when
  with one man manned.

John Donne, 'To His Mistress
Going to Bed' *(c.1595)* •927

i like my body when it is with your
body. It is so quite a new thing.
Muscles better and nerves more.
i like your body. i like what it does,
i like its hows.

e.e. cummings, 'Sonnets-Actualities'
no.8 *(1925)* •928

But did they feel the earth move?

Ernest Hemingway, For Whom
the Bell Tolls *(1940)* •929

Sex is more exciting on the
screen and between the pages
than between the sheets.

Andy Warhol, From A to B and
Back Again *(1975)* •930

Reading about sex in yesterday's novels is liking watching people smoke in old films.

*Novelist and scriptwriter Fay Weldon
in* the Guardian, *1 December 1989* •931

I've mostly written about sex by means of the space break.

Barbara Kingsolver, in Writers on Writing: Collected Essays from the New York Times *(2001)* •932

We have long past the Victorian era where asterisks were followed after a certain interval by a baby.

W. Somerset Maugham, The Constant Wife *(1926)* •933

Sex can be indicated with asterisks. I've always felt that was as good a way as any. *John Dos Passos, in* George Plimpton (ed.) The Writer's Chapbook *(1989)* •934

There is sex in the Discworld books, but it usually takes place two pages after the ending.

Terry Pratchett, in Terry Pratchett and Stephen Briggs, The Discworld Companion *(1994)* •935

Is it not strange that desire should so many years outlive performance?

William Shakespeare, Henry IV, Part 2 *(1597)* II.iv •936

193

Give me chastity and continency — but not yet!
St Augustine of Hippo, **Confessions** *(AD 397-8)* •937

Lolita, light of my life, fire of my loins My sin, my soul. *Vladimir Nabokov,* **Lolita** *(1955)* •940

What angel wakes me from my flowery bed?
Titania to Bottom, despite his ass's head, **A Midsummer Night's Dream III.i** *(1595)* •938

What is commonly called love, namely the desire of satisfying a voracious appetite with a certain quantity of delicate white human flesh.
Henry Fielding, **Tom Jones** *(1749)* •941

He was as fressh as is the month of May.
Chaucer, **The Canterbury Tales,** 'The General Prologue' •939

He in a few minutes ravished this fair creature, or at least would have ravished her, if she had not, by a timely compliance, prevented him.
Henry Fielding, **Jonathan Wild** *(1743)* •942

A little she strove, and
  much repented,
And whispering 'I will ne'er
  consent' — consented.

Lord Byron, **Don Juan** *(1819-24)* •943

The reading or non-reading
a book — will never keep
down a single petticoat.

Lord Byron, **letter to Richard Hoppner,**
29 October 1819 •944

Love ceases
to be pleasure
when it ceases
to be a secret.

English writer and adventuress
Aphra Behn •945

A mistress should be
like a little country retreat
near the town, not to dwell
in constantly, but only
for a night and away.

William Wycherley,
The Country Wife *(1675)* •946

Love is like linen; often
changed, the sweeter.

Phineas Fletcher, **Sicelides** *(performed 1614)* •947

How happy I could
  be with either,
Were t'other dear
  charmer away!

John Gay, **The Beggar's Opera**
(1728) •948

No visit to Dove Cottage, Grasmere, is complete without examining the outhouse where Hazlitt's father, a Unitarian minister of strong liberal views, attempted to put his hand up Dorothy Wordsworth's skirt.

Alan Coren •949

A lover without indiscretion is no lover at all.

Thomas Hardy,
The Hand of Ethelberta
(1876) •950

Food comes first, then morals.

Bertolt Brecht, Die Dreigroschenoper *(1928)* •951

Not to be born is,
past all prizing, best.

Sophocles, **Oedipus Coloneus** •952

Better is the end of a thing
than the beginning thereof.

Bible, Eccliesiastes 7.8 •953

Never to have lived is best, ancient writers say;

Never to have drawn the breath of life, never
to have looked into the eye of day;

The second best's a gay goodnight and
quickly turn away.

W.B.Yeats, **'From Oedipus at Colonus'**
(1928) •954

Birth, and copulation, and death.

That's all the facts when you come
to brass tacks:

Birth, copulation, and death.

I've been born, and once is enough.

T.S. Eliot, **Sweeney Agonistes** *(1932)* •955

Oh, isn't life
a terrible thing,
thank God?

Dylan Thomas, **Under Milk Wood** *(1954)* •956

Nothing happens,
nobody comes,
nobody goes, it's awful!

Samuel Beckett, **Waiting for Godot** *(1955)* •957

This world is a comedy to those that think, a tragedy to those that feel.

Horace Walpole, letter to Anne, Countess of Upper Ossory, *16 August 1776* •958

Laughter is pleasant, but the exertion is too much for me.

Thomas Love Peacock, Nightmare Abbey *(1818)* •959

Laugh and the world laughs with you, snore and you sleep alone.

Anthony Burgess, Inside Mr Enderby *(1968)* •960

The funniest thing about comedy is that you never know why people laugh. I know what makes them laugh but trying to get your hands on the why of it is like trying to pick an eel out of a tub of water.

W.C. Fields, in R.J. Anobile, A Flask of Fields *(1972)* •961

Comedy is an imitation of the common errors of our life.

Philip Sidney, The Defence of Poetry *(1595)* •962

Well there you are. This is life. What I've found as a writer is that you have to keep taming it down, making it less improbable in order to fit it into some sort of fictional context.

John Mortimer, in **Paris Review** *1995* •963

When Gregor Samsa awoke one morning from uneasy dreams he found himself transformed in his bed into a gigantic insect.

Franz Kafka, **The Metamorphosis** *(1915)* •964

A novel is balanced between a few true impressions and the multitude of false ones that make up the most of what we call life. It tells us that for every human being there is a diversity of existences, that the single existence is itself an illusion in part… it promises us meaning, harmony, and even justice.

Saul Bellow, speech on receiving the Nobel Prize 1976 •965

Imagination is not enough. Knowledge is necessary.

Paul Scott, in **Hilary Spurling, Paul Scott** *(1990)* •966

I distrust the incommunicable: it is the source of all violence.

Jean-Paul Sartre, 'Qu'est-ce que la littérature?' *in* **Les Temps Modernes** *July 1947* •967

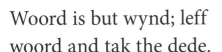

Woord is but wynd; leff woord and tak the dede.

John Lydgate, c.1370-c.1451, **Secrets of Old Philosophers** •968

Life, you know, is rather like opening a tin of sardines. We are all of us looking for the key. And, I wonder, how many of you here tonight have wasted years of your lives looking behind the kitchen dressers of this life for that key.

Alan Bennett, **Beyond the Fringe,** *(1961 revue)* 'Take a Pew' •969

It has long been an axiom of mine that the little things are infintely the most important.

Arthur Conan Doyle, **Adventures of Sherlock Holmes** *(1892)* •970

The only means of strengthening one's intellect is to make up one's mind about nothing — to let the mind be a thoroughfare for all my thoughts. Not a select party.

John Keats, **letter to George and Georgiana Keats,** *24 September 1819* •971

The test of a first-rate intelligence is the ability to hold two opposed ideas in the mind at the same time, and still retain the ability to function.

F. Scott Fitzgerald, in **Esquire** *February 1936,* 'The Crack-Up' •972

Pooh began to feel a little more comfortable, because when you are a Bear of Very Little Brain, and you Think of Things, you find sometimes that a Thing that seemed very Thingish inside you is quite different when it gets out in the open and has other people looking at it.

A.A. Milne, The House at Pooh Corner *(1928)* •973

All intellectual improvement arises from leisure.

Samuel Johnson, in Boswell, Life of Samuel Johnson *(1791)* •974

What is this life if, full of care,
We have no time to stand and stare?

W.H. Davies, 'Leisure' *(1911)* •975

If all the year were
    playing holidays,
To sport would be as
    tedious as to work;
But when they seldom come,
    they wished for come.

> *William Shakespeare,*
> Henry IV, Part I *(1597)* I.ii •976

Life's not just being alive, but being well.

Martial, AD c.40-c.104, Epigrammata •977

202

You should pray to have a sound mind in a sound body.

Juvenal, Satires •978

Noble deeds and hot baths are the best cures for depression.

Dodie Smith, I Capture the Castle *(1949)* •979

If a lot of cures are suggested for a disease, it means that the disease is incurable.

Anton Chekhov, The Cherry Orchard, Act.1 *(1904)* •980

I am but mad north-north-west; when the wind is southerly, I know a hawk from a handsaw.

William Shakespeare, Hamlet *(1601)* II.ii •981

I am never better than when I am mad. Then methinks I am a brave fellow; then I do wonders. But reason abuseth me, and there's the torment, there's the hell.

Thomas Kyd, The Spanish Tragedy *(1592)* The Fourth Addition •982

There is no greater sorrow than to recall a time of happiness.

Dante •983

For if the darkness and corruption
leave a vestige of the thoughts that
once I had, better by far you should
forget and smile than that you
should remember and be sad.

Poet Christina Rossetti,
'Remember', *1862* •984

The past is a foreign country;
they do things differently there.

L.P. Hartley, The Go-Between *(1953)* •985

Time present and
  time past
Are both perhaps
  present in time future
And time future
  contained in time past.

T.S. Eliot, Four Quartets
'Burnt Norton' *(1936)* •986

Truth is the most valuable thing we have. Let us economize it.

Mark Twain, Following the Equator *(1897)* •987

Tis strange — but true;
  for truth is always strange;
stranger than fiction.

Lord Byron, Don Juan *(1819-24)* •988

The truth is rarely pure, and never simple.
Oscar Wilde, The Importance of Being Earnest *(1895)* •989

What if this present were the world's last night?
John Donne, Holy Sonnets *(after 1609)* •990

All shall be well and all shall be well and all manner of things shall be well.
Julian of Norwich, 14th Century mystic, Revelations of Divine Love •991

Vladimir: That passed the time.
Estragon: It would have passed anyway.
Vladimir: Yes, but not so rapidly.

Samuel Beckett, Waiting for Godot *(1955)* •992

Sir, more than kisses, let us mingle souls.

John Donne, 'To Sir Henry Wotton' *(1597-8)*
•993

Know then thyself, presume
  not God to scan;

The proper study of mankind
  is man.

Alexander Pope, An Essay on Man —
Epistle 2 *(1733)* •994

Man is born to live,
not to prepare for life.

Boris Pasternak, Doctor Zhivago *(1958)* •996

People in life hardly
seem definite enough
to appear in print.

Ivy Compton-Burnett, attrib. in The
Times Literary Supplement *29 May 1982* •995

Youth, what man's age is like to be doth show;

We may our ends by our beginnings know.

John Denham, 'Of Prudence' *(1668)* •997

Men must be taught as if you
   taught them not,

And things unknown proposed
   as things forgot.

Alexander Pope, An Essay
on Criticism *(1711)* •998

He can't think
without his hat.

Samuel Beckett, Waiting for Godot
(1955) •999

Western culture… was a grand
ancestral property that educated
men inherited from their intellectual
forefathers, while their female relatives,
like characters in a Jane Austen novel,
were relegated to modest dower houses
on the edge of the estate.

Sandra M. Gilbert, 'What Do
Feminist Critics Want?' *(1980)* •1000

Men have had every advantage
of us in telling their own story.
Education has been theirs in so
much higher a degree; the pen
has been in their hands.

Jane Austen, Persuasion *(1818)* •1001

A man who moralises
is usually a hypocrite,
and a woman who moralises
is invariably plain.

Oscar Wilde, Lady Windermere's Fan,
(1892) •1002

Vice is detestable; I banish all its appearances from my coteries; and I would banish its reality, too, were I sure I should then have any thing but empty chairs in my drawing-room.
Fanny Burney, **Camilla** *(1796)* •1005

Conventionality is not morality. Self-righteousness is not religion. To attack the first is not to assail the last. To pluck the mask from the face of the Pharisee, is not to lift an impious hand to the Crown of Thorns.
Charlotte Brontë, **Jane Eyre** *(2nd ed., 1848)* **preface** •1003

Man is the Only Animal that Blushes. Or needs to.
Mark Twain, **Following the Equator** *(1897)* •1006

It is particularly encumbent on those who never change their opinion to be secure of judging properly at first.
Jane Austen, Lizzie Bennet in **Pride and Prejudice** •1004

Man is the only animal that laughs and weeps; for he is the only animal that is struck by the difference between what things are, and what they ought to be.
William Hazlitt, **Lectures on English Comic Writers** *(1818)* •1007

A tragic situation exists when virtue does not triumph but when it is still felt that man is nobler than the forces that destroy him.

George Orwell, 'Lear, Tolstoy and the Fool' *(1947)* •1008

Sport strips away personality, letting the white bone of character shine through.

Rita Mae Brown, **Sudden Death** *(1983)* •1009

What I know most surely about morality and the duty of man I owe to sport.

Albert Camus, in Herbert R. Lottman, **Albert Camus** *(1979)* •1010

Man is a history-making creature who can neither repeat his past nor leave it behind. *W.H. Auden,* The Dyer's Hand *(1962)* •1011

It is well to observe the force and virtue and consequence of discoveries, and these are to be seen nowhere more conspicuously than in those three which were unknown to the ancients, and of which the origins, though recent, are obscure and inglorious; namely, printing, gunpowder, and the mariner's needle [compass]. For these three have changed the whole face and state of things throughout the world.

Francis Bacon, **Novum Organum** *(1620)* •1012

How quick come the reasons for approving what we like!

Jane Austen, **Persuasion** •1013

At some time in the future, if the human mind becomes something totally different from what it now is, we may learn to separate literary creation from intellectual honesty. At present we know only that the imagination, like certain wild animals, will not breed in captivity.

George Orwell, 'The Prevention of Literature' *in* **Polemic,** *January 1946* •1014

We can't all be happy, we can't all be rich, we can't all be lucky... Some must cry so that others may be able to laugh the more heartily.

Jean Rhys, **Good Morning, Midnight** *(1939)* •1015

'Blessed is the man who expects nothing, for he shall never be disappointed' was the ninth beatitude.

Alexander Pope, **letter to Fortescue,** *23rd September 1725* •1016

From envy are born hatred, detraction, calumny, joy caused by the misfortune of a neighbour, and displeasure caused by his prosperity.

Gregory the Great •1017

211

Here's the rule for bargains: 'Do other men, for they would do you.' That's the true business precept.

Charles Dickens, Martin Chuzzlewit *(1844)* •1018

If you pick up a starving dog and make him prosperous, he will not bite you. That is the principal difference between a dog and a man.

Mark Twain •1019

We have just enough religion to make us hate, but not enough to make us love one another.

Jonathan Swift, Thoughts on Various Subjects *(1711)* •1020

I sometimes think God, in creating man, somewhat overestimated his ability. *Oscar Wilde.* •1021

Often it seems
a pity Noah
and his party
didn't miss
the boat.

Mark Twain •1022

Ah, but a man's reach
   should exceed his grasp,

Or what's a heaven for?

Robert Browning, 'Andrea del Sarto'
(1855) •1023

The lark's on the wing;
The snail's on the thorn:
God's in his heaven —
All's right with the world!

Robert Browning, **Pippa Passes** *(1841)* •1024

And this our life, exempt
from public haunt,

Finds tongues in trees,
books in running brooks,

Sermons in stones, and
good in everything.

William Shakespeare,
As You Like It *(1599)* •1025

There is a place in
the pathless woods,

There is a rapture on
the lonely shore,

There is a society, where
none intrudes,

By the deep sea,
and music in its roar:

I love not man the less,
but nature more.

Lord Byron, **Childe Harold's Pilgrimage**
(1812-18) •1026

After you have exhausted what
there is in business, politics,
conviviality, and so on — have
found that none of these finally
satisfy, or permanently wear —
what remains? Nature remains.

Walt Whitman, **Specimen Days
and Collect** *(1882)* •1027

Give me odorous at sunrise
a garden of beautiful flowers
where I can walk undisturbed.
Walt Whitman, Give Me the Splendid
Silent Sun *(pub. in* Leaves of Grass, *1900)*
•1028

People from a planet
without flowers would
think we must be mad
with joy the whole
time to have such
things about us.
Iris Murdoch, A Fairly Honourable
Defeat *(1970)* •1029

Summer afternoon —
summer afternoon… the
two most beautiful words
in the English language.
Henry James; in Edith Wharton,
A Backward Glance *(1934)* •1030

Just living is not enough…
One must have sunshine,
freedom, and a little flower.
Hans Christian Andersen •1031

The most beautiful things in
the world are the most useless
— peacocks and lilies for
instance.
John Ruskin •1032

While the earth remaineth,
seedtime and harvest, and
cold and heat, and summer
and winter, and day and
night shall not cease.
Bible, Genesis 8:22 •1033

'I play for Seasons; not Eternities!'
Says Nature.
George Meredith, **Modern Love** *(1862)* •1034

Gie me ae spark o' Nature's fire,
That's a' the learning I desire.
Robert Burns, **'First Epistle to Lapraik'**
(1785) •1035

All good things are artificial, for nature is the art of God.

Sir Thomas Browne, **Religio Medici** *(1643)*
•1036

She had never seen a place of which nature had done more, or where natural beauty had been so little counteracted by an awkward taste.

Jane Austen, **Pride & Prejudice.** *Elizabeth's first view of Pemberley, believed to be based on Chatsworth House.* •1037

Nothing is more the child of art than a garden.

Sir Walter Scott •1038

Man masters nature not by force but by understanding.

English poet and dramatist
Robert Bridges, **attr.** •1039

Trees sing and dance, make faces and give flower bouquets, trying to be loved. You ever notice that trees do everything to get attention we do, except walk? *Alice Walker,*
The Color Purple •1040

No matter how often you knock at nature's door, she won't answer in words you can understand — for Nature is dumb. She'll vibrate and moan like a violin, but you mustn't expect a song.
Ivan Turgenev, **On the Eve** (1860) •1041

'We can talk,' said the Tiger-lily, 'when there's anybody worth talking to.'
Lewis Carroll, **Through the Looking-Glass** (1872) •1042

But when Beryl looked at the bush, it seemed to her the bush was sad. We are dumb trees, reaching up in the night, imploring we know not what, said the sorrowful bush.
Katherine Mansfield,
'The Garden Party' (1922) •1043

I have learned
To look on nature, not as in the hour
Of thoughtless youth; but hearing often-times
The still, sad music of humanity.
William Wordsworth, **'Lines composed a few miles above Tintern Abbey'** (1798) •1044

Nature is unforgiving; she will not agree to withdraw her flowers, her music, her scents or her rays of light before the abominations of man.
Victor Hugo, **Ninety-three** (1874) •1045

The best remedy for those who are afraid, lonely or unhappy is to go outside, somewhere where they can be quiet, alone with the heavens, nature and God. Because only then does one feel that all is as it should be...

Anne Frank, The Diary of Anne Frank *(1947)* •1046

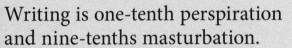

Writing is one-tenth perspiration
and nine-tenths masturbation.

Alan Bennett •1047

89% work and worry over work, struggle against lunacy 10%, and friends 1%.

Tennessee Williams with a breakdown of his life; John Lahr, Light Fantastic *(1996)*
•1048

Writing is not a profession but a vocation of unhappiness.

Georges Simenon; interview in Paris Review, *1955* •1049

Only amateurs say they write for their own amusement. Writing is not an amusing occupation. It is a combination of ditch-digging, mountain-climbing, treadmill and childbirth. Writing may be interesting, absorbing, exhilarating, racking, relieving. But amusing? Never!

Edna Ferber, A Peculiar Treasure *(1939)* •1050

How one likes to suffer. Anyway writers do; it is their income.

W.H. Auden, Berlin diary, *April 1929* •1051

I am a galley slave to pen and ink.

Honoré de Balzac, letter *1832* •1052

It was labour-intensive work, scriptorium-slow.
Seamus Heaney on translating Beowulf; Beowulf *(1999)* **Introduction** •1053

It bored me hellishly to write the Emigrant; well, it's going to bore others to read it; that's only fair.
Robert Louis Stevenson, letter to Sidney Colvin, *January 1880* •1054

Three hours a day will produce as much as a man ought to write.
Anthony Trollope, Thackeray *(1879)* •1055

You know, it's not exactly a natural pursuit, a man putting himself in front of a typewriter — a machine — day after day. But you've got to spend three or four years digging yourself a rut so deep that finally you find it more convenient not to get out of it. *Ernest Haycox, in* **Ernest Haycox** *(1996)* •1056

Only habit of persistent work can make one continually content; it produces an opium that numbs the soul.
Gustave Flaubert, Letter *26 July 1851* •1057

221

Nature is monstrously unjust.
There is no substitute for talent.
Industry and all the virtues
are of no avail.

Aldous Huxley, in **George Greenfield,
Scribblers for Bread** *(1989)* •1058

The solitary genius in the garret
is a male myth, as he would
undoubtedly have been supported
by several unacknowledged
women who cooked and ironed.

Michèle Roberts, in **Independent on
*Sunday 4 February 1996*** •1059

Literature cannot be the
business of a woman's life,
because of the sacredness
of her duties at home.

Robert Southey on Charlotte Brontë •1060

Only ambitious nonentities
and hearty mediocrities
exhibit their rough drafts.
It's like passing around
samples of one's sputum.

Vladimir Nabokov •1061

The pleasure of the first draft
lies in deceiving yourself that
it is quite close to the real thing.
The pleasure of the subsequent
drafts lies partly in realizing
that you haven't been gulled by
the first draft. *Julian Barnes, in* **Paris
Review** *Winter 2000* •1062

222

It's nice to have company when you come face to face with a blank page.

George S. Kaufman on collaboration, in Howard Teichman, George S. Kaufman: an Intimate Portrait *(1973)* •1063

No man but a blockhead ever wrote, except for money.
Samuel Johnson, in Boswell, Life of Samuel Johnson *(1791) 5 April 1776* •1064

The profession of letters is, after all, the only one in which one can make no money without being ridiculous.

Jules Renard, Diary *1906* •1065

Were I my own man… I would refuse this offer (with all gratitude); but as I am situated, £300 or £400 a-year is not to be sneezed at.

Sir Walter Scott sees the value of the Laureateship; letter to James Ballantyne, 24 August 1813 •1066

I'm a jobbing writer, like everyone else.

Fay Weldon on why she agreed to write a product-placement novel commissioned by a jewellery company. •1067

Some day I hope to write a book where the royalties will pay for the copies I give away.

Clarence Darrow, American lawyer •1068

Crime does not pay — enough.

Clayton Rawson, founder of Mystery Writers of America; in **American Heritage Dictionary of American Quotations** *(1997)* •1069

My object is renumeration.

Frances Hodgson Burnett, submitting her first short story for magazine publication; **letter** *c.1867* •1070

For me I never cared for fame
Solvency was my only aim.

British poet and editor J.C. Squire, at a dinner given in his honour, 15 December 1932 •1071

Many books are written…for very mundane reasons. It tends to be forgotten, for example, that Johnson wrote Rasselas to defray the expenses of his mother's funeral, or that Dumas's terse, interrogative dialogue was the result of his being paid at so many centimes a line.   *D.J. Taylor,*
After the War *(1993)* •1072

Write without pay until somebody offers you pay. If nobody offers within three years the candidate may look upon the circumstance with the most implicit confidence as the sign that sawing wood is what he was intended for.

Mark Twain •1073

Just try doing your VAT return
with a head full of goblins.

*Terry Pratchett on whether he lives in
his fantasy world.* •1074

I have just received
nearly twenty pounds
myself on the second
edition of 'Sense and
Sensibility' which gives
me a fine flow of
literary ardour.

Jane Austen •1075

It's about to make me rich.

*Tom Stoppard, in response to the question
'what is* Rosencrantz and Guildenstern are
Dead *about?' after its first night in New York;
in* Independent *2 December 1995* •1076

All you need in life is ignorance
and confidence; then success is sure.

Mark Twain, **letter to Mrs Foote,** *2 December 1887* •1077

Modern fame is too often a
crown of thorns, and brings
all the vulgarity of the world
upon you. I sometimes wish
I had never written a line.

*Alfred, Lord Tennyson, in conversation
with Marie Corelli;* **Theresa Ransom, The
Mysterious Miss Marie Corelli** *(1999)* •1079

It took me fifteen years to
discover I had no talent for
writing, but I couldn't give
it up because by that time
I was too famous.

Robert Benchley, quoted in **Robert
Benchley, by Nat Benchley,** *1955,* •1078

Celebrity is a
mask that eats
into the face.

John Updike, **Self-Consciousness:
Memoirs** *(1989)* •1080

The best fame is a writer's fame: it's enough to get a table at a good restaurant, but not enough that you get interrupted when you eat.
Fran Lebowitz, in Observer *30 May 1993,* 'Sayings of the Week' •1081

The usual drawback to success is that it annoys one's friends so.
P.G. Wodehouse, 'The Man Upstairs', *(1914)* •1082

For a writer, success is always temporary, success is only a delayed failure. And it is incomplete.
Graham Greene, A Sort of Life *(1931)* •1083

The common idea that success spoils people by making them vain, egotistic, and self-complacent is erroneous; on the contrary it makes them, for the most part, humble, tolerant, and kind. Failure makes people bitter and cruel.
W. Somerset Maugham, The Summing Up *(1938)* •1084

Fools admire everything in a respected author.
Voltaire, Candide *(1759)* •1085

Even for learned men, love of fame is the last thing to be given up.

Tacitus, Histories •1086

I should so much have loved to be popular!

Henry James, in Alfred Sutro Celebrities and Simple Souls *(1933)*•1087

A best-seller was a book which somehow sold well simply because it was selling well.

US librarian, historian, lawyer and writer Daniel Boorstin, The Image *(1962)* •1088

A best-seller is the gilded tomb of a mediocre talent.

Logan Pearsall Smith, Afterthoughts *(1931)* •1089

My Rome praises my little books, loves them, recites them; I am in every pocket, every hand. *Martial,* Epigrammata •1090

228

When one says that
a writer is fashionable
one practically always
means that he is admired
by people under thirty.
George Orwell •1091

In America only the successful
writer is important, in France
all writers are important, in
England no writer is important,
in Australia you have to
explain what a writer is.
Geoffrey Cotterell, New York Journal, *1961* •1093

'The Ancient Mariner' would
not have taken so well if it had
been called 'The Old Sailor'.
Samuel Butler (1835-1902), attrib. •1092

Ever tried. Ever failed.
No matter. Try again.
Fail again. Fail better.
Samuel Beckett, Worstward Ho *(1983)* •1094

No author is a man of genius to his publisher.

Heinrich Heine, German Poet. •1095

I object to publishers: the one service they have done me is to teach me to do without them. They combine commercial rascality with artistic touchiness and pettiness, without being either good business men or fine judges of literature.

George Bernard Shaw •1096

An editor is one who separates the wheat from the chaff and prints the chaff.

> *Adlai Stevenson,*
> **The Stevenson Wit** *(1966)* •1097

Everywhere I go I'm asked if I think the universities stifle writers. My opinion is that they don't stifle enough of them. There's many a best-seller that could have been prevented by a good teacher.

Flannery O'Connor, in
The Writer's Craft *(1974)* •1098

All a publisher has to do is write cheques at intervals, while a lot of deserving and industrious chappies rally round and do the real work.

P.G. Wodehouse, **My Man Jeeves** *(1919)* •1099

There is only one way to make money at writing, and that is to marry a publisher's daughter.
George Orwell, **Down and Out in Paris and London** *(1933)* •1100

Publishing is not ordinary trade: it is gambling. The publisher bets the cost of manufacturing, advertising and circulating a book, plus the overhead of his establishment, against every book he publishes exactly as a turf bookmaker bets against every horse in the race.
George Bernard Shaw, in **The Author,** Summer *1945* •1101

Our Grubstreet biographers watch for the death of a great man, like so many undertakers, on purpose to make a penny out of him. *Joseph Addison,* **Freeholder** *(1715-16)* •1102

There's never been much love lost between literature and the market. The consumer economy loves a product that sells at a premium, wears out quickly or is susceptible to regular improvement… A classic work of literature is inexpensive, infinitely re-usable, and, worst of all, unimprovable. *Jonathan Franzen,* **How to be Alone?** *(2002)* **'Why bother?'** •1103

231

Though our publishers will tell you that they are ever seeking 'original writers', nothing could be farther from the truth. What they want is more of the same, only thinly disguised…What the public wants, no one knows. Not even the publishers.

Henry Miller, 'When I Reach for My Revolver' *(1955)* •1104

The shelf-life of the modern hardback writer is somewhere between the milk and the yoghurt.

Calvin Trillin, in The Sunday Times *9 June 1991;* **attrib.** •1105

Good editors are really the third eye. Cool. Dispassionate. They don't love you or your work; for me that is what is valuable — not compliments. Sometimes it's uncanny; the editor puts his or her finger on exactly the place the writer knows is weak…

Toni Morrison, in Women Writers at Work: Paris Review Interviews *(1998)* •1106

[The editor] should say to himself, 'How can I help this writer to say it better in his own style?' and avoid 'How can I show him how I would write it, if it were my piece?'

James Thurber in a memo to New Yorker *in 1959, reprinted in* New York Times Book Review *4 December 1988* •1107

You cannot or at least should not try to argue with authors. Too many are like children whose tears can suddenly be changed to smiles if they are handled in the right way.

A publisher's view from Michael Joseph, The Adventure of Publishing *(1949)* •1108

I've had great fun doing some stories by phone with certain magazine editors… Bargaining goes on, horse-trading. 'You can have the dash if I can get the semicolon.'

Margaret Atwood, in an interview, March 1986; in **Paris Review** *Winter 1990* •1109

No need to change the title. Easier to change publishers.

Graham Greene, in a telegram to his American publishers after they responded to the manuscript of his **Travels with my Aunt** *with 'Terrific book, but we'll need to change the title.'* •1110

Never buy an editor or publisher a lunch or a drink until he has bought an article story or book from you. This rule is absolute and may be broken only at your peril.

John Creasey, British crime writer. •1111

The author's agent fosters in authors the greed for an immediate money return… at the cost of all dignity and repose.

William Heinemann, in **The Author,** *c.1890 — in George Greenfield,* **Scribblers for Bread** *(1989)* •1112

Talking of agents, when I opened the morning paper one morning last week I saw that it had finally happened: somebody shot one. It was probably for the wrong reasons but at least it was a step in the right direction.

Raymond Chandler, **letter to Charles Morton** *17 December 1951* •1113

A good many young writers make the mistake of enclosing a stamped, self-addressed envelope, big enough for the manuscript to come back in. This is too much of a temptation to the editor.

Ring Lardner, **How to Write Short Stories** *(1924)* **preface** •1114

233

My story 'The Sea and Its Shore' came back from The Criterion with two rejection slips enclosed, which seems unnecessarily cruel.

Elizabeth Bishop, **letter to Marianne Moore,** *25 February 1937* •1115

I have an exceedingly odd sensation, when I consider that… a work which was so lately lodged in all privacy, in my bureau may now be seen by every butcher and baker, cobbler and tinker, throughout the three kingdoms, for the small tribute of three pence.

Fanny Burney on the perils of publication; **Diary,** *March 1778* •1117

The book of my enemy has been remaindered And I am pleased.

Brian James, Australian writer; 'The Book of My Enemy Has Been Remaindered' •1116

I will carry on writing, to be sure. But I don't know if I would want to publish again.

J.K. Rowling, author of the **Harry Potter** *Books.* •1118

Publish and be damned.

Duke Of Wellington's reply to a threat of blackmail from Harriette Wilson, c.1825; **attrib** •1119

A merchant shall
hardly keep himself
from doing wrong.

Bible, Ecclesiastes 26.29 •1122

If possible honestly,
if not somehow,
make money.

Horace, **Epistles** •1120

Get place and wealth,
if possible, with grace;

If not, by any means get
wealth and place.

Alexander Pope, **Imitations of
Horace** *(1738)* •1121

Money, which represents the prose of
life, and which is hardly spoken of in
parlours without an apology, is, in its
effects and laws, as beautiful as roses.

Ralph Waldo Emerson,
Essays, Second Series *(1844)*
'Nominalist and Realist' •1123

A large income is the best recipe for happiness I ever heard of.

Jane Austen, Mary Crawford in **Mansfield Park** *(1814)* •1124

We are all Adam's children but silk makes the difference.

Thomas Fuller, **Gnomologia** *(1732)* •1125

A single woman, with a very narrow income, must be a ridiculous disagreeable old maid! the proper sport of boys and girls; but a single woman of good fortune, is always respectable, and may be sensible and pleasant as anybody else.

Jane Austen, Emma in **Emma** *(1815)* •1126

Business, you know, may bring money, but friendship hardly ever does.

Jane Austen, Mr Knightley in **Emma** *(1815)*•1127

It is very difficult for the prosperous to be humble.

Jane Austen, Frank Churchill in **Emma** *(1815)* •1128

Plenty has made me poor.

Ovid, **Metamorphoses** •1129

But there are certainly not so many men of large fortune in the world as there are pretty women to deserve them.

Jane Austen, **Mansfield Park** *(1814)* •1130

Money can only give
happiness where there
is nothing else to give.
Jane Austen, Marianne in
Sense and Sensibility *(1811)* •1131

We all need money, but there
are degrees of desperation.
Anthony Burgess, in **Face,** *December 1984* •1132

All decent people live
beyond their incomes
nowadays, and those
who aren't respectable
live beyond other peoples'.

Saki, **Chronicles of Clovis** *(1911)* •1133

Annual income twenty pounds, annual
expenditure nineteen and six: result happiness.
Annual income twenty pounds, annual expenditure
twenty pounds and six: result misery.
***Charles Dickens,* David Copperfield** *(1850)* •1134

I can get no remedy against
this consumption of the purse:
borrowing only lingers and
lingers it out, but the disease
is incurable. *William Shakespeare,*
Henry IV, Part 2 *(1597)* **I.ii**
•1135

Dreading that climax of all human ills,
The inflammation of his weekly bills.
Lord Byron, **Don Juan** *(1819-24)* •1136

Economy is going without something you do want in case you should, some day, want something you probably won't want. *Anthony Hope,* **The Dolly Dialogues** *(1894)* •1137

I'm tired of Love: I'm still more
  tired of Rhyme.
But Money gives me pleasure
  all the time.

   Hillaire Belloc, 'Fatigued' (1923) •1138

238

For forms of government let fools contest;
Whate'er is best administered is best.

Alexander Pope, An Essay on Man,
Epistle 3 •1139

I would not give half a guinea to live under one form of government than another. It is of no moment to the happiness of an individual.

Samuel Johnson, in Boswell,
Life of Samuel Johnson *(1791),*
31 March 1772 •1140

An election is coming. Universal peace is declared, and the foxes have a sincere interest in prolonging the lives of the poultry.

George Eliot,
Felix Holt *(1866)* •1141

In mobilising support for a project or policy it is especially agreeable to be able to call upon the distinguished dead; their distinction adds intellectual weight and moral force to the argument, and their death makes it impossible for them to appear on television later and say that they meant something completely different. *Antony Jay,*
introduction to Oxford Dictionary of Political Quotations *(1996)* •1142

No writer before the middle of the 19th century wrote about the working classes other than as grotesque or as pastoral decoration. Then when they were given the vote certain writers started to suck up to them. *Evelyn Waugh, in* Paris Review *1963* •1143

Political language… is designed to make lies sound truthful and murder respectable, and to give an appearance of solidity to pure wind. *George Orwell,* **Shooting an Elephant** *(1950)* **'Politics and the English Language'** •1144

My faith in the people governing is, on the whole, infinitesimal; my faith in The People governed is, on the whole, illimitable.

Charles Dickens, speech at Birmingham and Midland Institute, 27 September 1869 •1145

Good people do not need laws to tell them to act responsibly, while bad people will find a way around the laws.

Plato •1146

Good laws, if they are not obeyed, do not constitute good government.

Aristotle •1147

More laws, less justice.

Cicero •1148

The more corrupt the state, the more numerous the laws.

Tacitus •1149

The rusty curb of old father antick, the law.

William Shakespeare, **Henry IV, Part I** *(1597) I.ii* •1150

People must not do things for fun. We are not here for fun. There is no reference to fun in any Act of Parliament.

A.P. Herbert, **Uncommon Law** *(1935)* •1151

'If the law supposes that,' said Mr Bumble… 'the law is a ass — a idiot.'

Charles Dickens, **Oliver Twist** *(1838)* •1152

The one great principle of the English law is, to make business for itself. *Charles Dickens,*
Bleak House *(1853)* •1153

The law is reason free from passion.
Aristotle •1154

It seems to me the mark of a civilised society is that certain privileges should be taken for granted such as education, health care and the safety to walk the streets.
Alan Bennett •1155

Because it is difficult to join them together, it is much safer for a prince to be feared than loved, if he is to fail in one of the two.
Niccolò Machiavelli, **The Prince** *(written 1513)* •1156

Men of power have no time to read; yet the men who do not read are unfit for power.
Michael Foot •1157

Dictators are as scared of books as they are of cannon.
Harry Golden, **Only in America** *(1958)* •1158

Laws are silent in time of war.

Cicero, **Pro Milone** •1159

Force, and fraud, are in war the two cardinal virtues.

Thomas Hobbes, **Leviathan** *(1651)* •1160

War is capitalism with the gloves off and many who go to war know it but they go to war because they don't want to be a hero.

Tom Stoppard, **Travesties** *(1975)* •1162

BATTLE, n., A method of untying with the teeth a political knot that would not yield to the tongue.

Ambrose Bierce, **The Cynic's Word Book** *(1906)* •1161

How is the world ruled and led to war? Diplomats lie to journalists and believe these lies when they seem them in print.

Karl Kraus, **Nachts** *(1918)* •1163

'My country, right or wrong'
is a thing no patriot would think
of saying except in a
desperate case. It is like saying,
'My mother drunk or sober'.
G.K. Chesterton,
Defendant, *1901.* •1164

Dulce et decorum est pro patria
mori. — It is sweet and fitting
to die for one's country.
Horace, **Odes** •1165

If you could hear, at every jolt,
  the blood

Come gargling from the
  froth-corrupted lungs,

Obscene as cancer, bitter
  as the cud

Of vile, incurable sores
  on innocent tongues, —

My friend, you would not tell
  with such high zest

To children ardent for some
  desperate glory,

The old Lie: Dulce et decorum est
Pro patria mori.

> *Wilfred Owen,*
> **'Dulce et Decorum Est'**
> *(1918)* •1166

An author's first
duty is to let
down his country.

Brendan Behan,
The Guardian, *1960* •1167

Who live under the shadow of a war,

What can I do that matters?

Stephen Spender, **'Who live under**
the shadow of a war' *(1933)* •1168

I am a soldier, convinced that I am acting
on behalf of soldiers. I believe that this war,
upon which I entered as a war of defence and
liberation, has now become a war of aggression
and conquest. I believe that the purposes for
which I and my fellow-soldiers entered upon
this war should have been clearly stated as to
have made it impossible to change them, and
that, had this been done, the objects which
actuated us would now be attainable
by negotiation.

Siegfried Sassoon, **'A Soldier's Declaration'**
addressed to his commanding officer and
sent to **The Bradford Pioneer** *July 1917* •1169

What passing-bells for those
  who die as cattle?

Only the monstrous anger of
  the guns.

Only the stuttering rifles'
  rapid rattle

Can patter out their
  hasty orisons.

Poet Wilfred Owen, **'Anthem for**
Doomed Youth', *1917.* •1170

God is on the side
not of the heavy
battalions, but
of the best shots.

Voltaire, **'The Piccini Notebooks'** *(c.1735-50)*
•1171

Was none who would be foremost
To lead such dire attack;
But those behind cried 'Forward!'
And those before cried 'Back!'
Lord Macaulay, '**Horatius**' *(1842)* •1172

Once more unto the breach,
  dear friends, once more;
Or close up the wall with our
  English dead!
In peace there's nothing so
  becomes a man
As modest stillness and humility:
But when the blast of war blows
  in our ears,
Then imitate the action of the tiger;
Stiffen the sinews, summon
  up the bloody,
Disguise fair nature with
  hard-favoured rage;
Then lend the eye a terrible aspect.
                 William Shakespeare,
         Henry V *(1599)* **III.i** •1173

He saith among the trumpets, Ha ha; and he smelleth the battle afar off, the thunder of the captains, and the shouting. Bible, Job 39:25 •1174

See, the conquering hero comes!
Sound the trumpets, beat the drums!
English librettist Thomas Morell,
Judas Maccabeus *(1747)* •1175

Every man thinks meanly of himself for not having been a soldier, or not having been at sea.

Samuel Johnson, in Boswell's Life of Johnson *(1791), 10 April 1778* •1176

You can always tell an old soldier by the inside of his holsters and cartridge boxes. The young ones carry pistols and cartridges; the old ones, grub.

George Bernard Shaw, **Arms and the Man** *(1898)* •1177

As a general rule television is better than words in newspapers at communicating wars, and words are better than television at communicating peace.

Nicholas Tomalin, in The Listener *29 April 1971* •1178

So you're the little woman who wrote the book that made this great war!

Abraham Lincoln on meeting Harriet Beecher Stowe; attrib. •1179

The real war will never get in the books. And so goodbye to the war.

Walt Whitman, writing after the American Civil War; Specimen Days *(1882)* 'The Real War Will Never Get in the Books' •1180

We make war that we may live in peace.
Aristotle, **Nicomachean Ethics** •1181

War always finds a way.
Bertolt Brecht, **Mother Courage** *(1939)* •1182

Beneath the rule of men entirely great
The pen is mightier than the sword.
George Bulwer-Lytton, **Richelieu** *(1839)* •1183

Books cannot be killed by fire. People die, but books never die. No man and no force can abolish memory… In this war, we know, books are weapons. And it is a part of your dedication always to make them weapons for man's freedom.
Franklin D. Roosevelt, 'Message to the Booksellers of America' *6 May 1942* •1184

A good newspaper, I suppose, is a nation talking to itself.
Arthur Miller, in The Observer
26 November 1961 •1185

All a poet can do today is warn.
Wilfred Owen; **preface** *(written 1918)* **in** Poems *(1963)* •1186

Nothing I wrote in the thirties saved one Jew from Auschwitz.

W.H. Auden, attrib. •1187

Whenever books will be burned, men also, in the end, are burned.

Heinrich Heine, Almansor *(1823)* •1188

I disapprove of what you say, but I will defend to the death your right to say it.

Voltaire's attitude towards Helvetius following the burning of the latter's De l'esprit *in 1759. Attributed to Voltaire, the words are in fact S.G. Tallentyre's summary in* The Friends of Voltaire *(1907)* •1189

Freedom of the press is guaranteed only to those who own one.

A.J. Liebling, 'The Wayward Press: Do you belong in Journalism?' *(1960)* •1190

A censor is a man who knows more than he thinks you ought to.

Laurence J. Peter, Canadian educator known for his 'Peter Principle', attrib. *1982* •1191

I dislike censorship. Like an appendix it is useless when inert and dangerous when active. *Politician and novelist Maurice Edelman,* attrib. *1982* •1192

It takes away any desire you have
to express yourself freely; whenever
you write, you get a feeling there's
a bone stuck in your throat.

Anton Chekhov on Russian censorship,
letter *19 January 1895* •1193

I suppose that writers should,
in a way, feel flattered by the
censorship laws. They show
a primitive fear and dread
at the fearful magic of print.

John Mortimer, **Clinging to the Wreckage**
(1982) •1194

It would be absurd
to think that a book
can cause riots.

*Salman Rushdie, to Indian interviewer in
September 1988; his book* The Satanic Verses
invoked a fatwah against him. In Sunday
Times *23 July 1989* •1195

To be arrested for the power of
your writing is one of the highest
compliments an author can be
paid, if an unwelcome one.

*Kenyan author Ngugi wa Thiong'o on being
imprisoned without trial, in 1977;* **attrib.** •1196

What is a rebel?
A man who says no.

Albert Camus, L'Homme révolté *(1951)* •1197

The men who ordained and supervised this show of shame, this tragic charade, are frightened by the word, the power of ideas, the power of the pen… They are so scared of the word that they do not read. And that will be their funeral.

Nigerian writer and activist Ken Saro-Wiwa, shortly before his execution in 1995; in London Review of Books *4 April 1996* •1198

The bravest are surely those who have the clearest vision of what is before them, glory and danger alike, and yet notwithstanding, go out to meet it.

Thucydides •1199

Lord take my soul, but the struggle continues.

Last words of Ken Saro-Wiwa before he was hanged; in The Daily Telegraph *13 November 1995* •1200

252

A word, in a word, is complicated.

Steven Pinker, The Language Instinct *(1994)* •1261

Words are, of course, the most powerful drug used by mankind.

Rudyard Kipling, speech, *14 February 1923*
•1262

Words are undervalued as a means of expression. Pictures tend to trivialise experience.

Arthur Miller, attrib., *1990* •1263

Wordstruck is exactly what I was — and still am: crazy about the sound of words, the look of words, the taste of words, the feeling for words on the tongue and in the mind.

Robert MacNeil, Wordstruck *(1989)* •1264

When I feel inclined to read poetry I take down my Dictionary. The poetry of words is quite as beautiful as that of sentences. The author may arrange the gems effectively, but their shape and lustre have been given by the attrition of ages.

> *Oliver Wendell Holmes,*
> The Autocrat of the
> Breakfast Table *(1858)* •1265

What a comfort a Dictionary is!

Lewis Carroll, Sylvie and Bruno Concluded *(1893)* •1266

We talk about the tyranny of words, but we like to tyrannise over them too; we are fond of having a large superfluous establishment of words to wait upon us on great occasions; we think it looks important, and sounds well.

Charles Dickens,
David Copperfield *(1850)* •1267

A definition is the enclosing a wilderness of ideas within a wall of words.

Samuel Butler (1835-1902),
Notebooks *(1912)* •1268

Words are like leaves; and where they most abound

Much fruit of sense beneath is rarely found.

Alexander Pope, **An Essay on Criticism** *(1711)* •1269

Continual eloquence is tedious.

Blaise Pascal, **Pensées** *(1670)* •1270

I fear those big words, Stephen said, which make us so unhappy.

James Joyce, **Ulysses** *(1922)* •1271

Et semel emissum volat
irrevocabile verbum. —
And once sent out a word
takes wing beyond recall.
Horace, Epistles •1272

Oaths are but words,
and words but wind.
Samuel Butler, Hudibras pt.2 *(1664)* •1273

Words are chameleons,
which reflect the colour
of their environment.
Learned Hand, in Commissioner v.
National Carbide Corp. *(1948)* •1274

When I cannot see
words curling like
rings of smoke round
me I am in darkness —
I am nothing.
Virginia Woolf, The Waves *(1931)* •1275

The limits of my language
mean the limits of my world.
Ludwig Wittgenstein, Tractatus Logico
Philosophicus *(1922)* •1276

The unconscious
is structured
like a language.
Jacques Lacan, Escrits *(1966)* •1277

Language can… be compared with a sheet of paper: thought is the front and sound the back; one cannot cut the front without cutting the back at the same time.

Ferdinand de Saussure, **Course in General Linguistics** *(1916)* •1278

An irony is a nipping jest, or a speech that hath the honey of pleasantness in its mouth, and a sting of rebuke in its tail.

Edward Reyner, **Rules for the Government of the Tongue** *(1656)* •1279

He gave man speech, and speech created thought,

Which is the measure of the universe.

> *Percy Bysshe Shelley,*
> **Prometheus Unbound**
> *(1820)* •1280

Language is the dress of thought.

Samuel Johnson, **Lives of the English Poets** *(1779-81)* •1281

She understood, as women do more easily than men, that the declared meaning of a spoken sentence is only its overcoat, and the real meaning lies underneath its scarves and buttons.

Peter Carey, **Oscar and Lucinda** *(1989)* •1282

257

He makes language
as physical as a bruise.

John Carey on Ted Hughes;
The Sunday Times
9 December 1979 •1283

Good heavens! For more than
forty years I have been speaking
prose without knowing it.

Molière, **Le Bourgeois Gentilhomme** *(1671)*
•1284

Slang is, at least, vigorous
and apt. Probably most
of our vital words
were once slang.

*John Galsworthy, in his presidential
address to the English Association in 1924;*
Castles in Spain and Other Screeds *(1927)*
•1285

Slang is language that rolls
up its sleeves, spits on its
hands and goes to work.

Carl Sandburg, in **The New York Times**
13 Febraury 1959 •1286

Remember that you are
a human being with a
soul and the divine gift
of articulate speech; that your
native language is the language of Shakespeare and
Milton and The Bible; and
don't sit there crooning like a
bilious pigeon.

George Bernard Shaw, **Pygmalion** *(1916)* •1287

Correct English is the slang of prigs who write history and essays. And the strongest slang of all is the slang of poets.

George Eliot, Middlemarch *(1871-2)* •1288

Stylists used to revere 'pure' English, but in reality English is about as pure as a factory effluent, and has displayed its mongrel toughness over the centuries by cannibalising a picturesque array of foreign tongues from Greek to Polynesian.

John Carey, in The Sunday Times *27 January 1985* •1289

So now they have made our English tongue a gallimaufry or hodgepodge of all other speeches.

Edmund Spenser, The Shepheard's Calendar *(1579)* •1290

They spell it Vinci and pronounce it Vinchy; foreigners always spell better than they pronounce.

Mark Twain, The Innocents Abroad *(1869)* •1291

Humour is the first of the gifts to perish in a foreign tongue.

Virginia Woolf, The Common Reader *(1st series, 1925)* 'On Not Knowing Greek' •1292

To speak English, one must place the tongue between the teeth, and I have lost my teeth.

Voltaire, to James Boswell, 24 December 1764; in Pottle (ed.) Boswell on the Grand Tour *(1953)* •1293

[The] collective unconscious of the race is the OED.

James Merrill, in American Poetry Review, *September/October 1979* 'On James Merrill' •1294

In my view, the greatest achievement of these islands was not arrived at by an individual, and not imagined by a single genius, but created, honed and sustained by millions over the centuries: the English language.

Melvyn Bragg, in The Observer *24 November 2002* •1295

Grammer, the ground of al.

William Langland, c.1330-c.1400, The Vision of Piers Plowman •1296

The notion 'grammatical' cannot be identified with 'meaningful' or 'significant' in any semantic sense. Sentences (1) and (2) are equally nonsensical, but… only the former is grammatical.
(1) Colourless green ideas sleep furiously.
(2) Furiously sleep ideas green colourless.

Noam Chomsky, Syntactic Structures *(1957)* •1297

My mother pointed out… that one could not say 'a green great dragon', but had to say 'a great green dragon.' I wondered why, and still do.

J.R.R. Tolkien on his first forays into storywriting, aged seven; **letter to W.H. Auden,** *7 June 1955* •1298

Would you convey my compliments to the purist who reads your proofs and tell him or her that I write in a sort of broken-down patois which is something like the way a Swiss waiter talks, and that when I split an infinitive, God damn it, I split it so it will stay split.

Raymond Chandler, **letter to Edward Weeks,** *18 January 1947* •1300

They've a temper, some of them — particularly verbs: they're the proudest — adjectives you can do anything with, but not verbs — however, I can manage the whole lot of them!

Lewis Carroll, **Through the Looking-Glass** *(1872)* •1299

The failure of English masters, at all the schools I attended, to give me any comprehension of the purpose of punctuation is splendidly evident in that story.

Angus Wilson, regarding his first short story, **'Raspberry Jam'** *(1946); in* **The Wild Garden** *(1963)* •1301

Punctuation ought to be exact. Under ordinary circumstances, it is as hard for me to alter punctuation as to alter words, though I will admit that at times I am heady and irresponsible. *Marianne Moore,* letter to Ezra Pound, *19 January 1919* •1302

My spelling is Wobbly. It's good spelling but it Wobbles, and the letters get in the wrong places. *A.A. Milne,* Winnie-the-Pooh *(1926)* •1304

Cut out all those exlamation marks. An exclamation mark is like laughing at your own joke.

F. Scott Fitzgerald, in Beloved Infidel *(1959)* •1303

The cure for mixed metaphors is for the patient to be obliged to draw a picture of the result. *Bernard Levin* •1305

Whenever the literary German dives into a sentence, that is the last you are going to see of him till he emerges on the other side of the Atlantic with his verb in his mouth.

Mark Twain, **A Connecticut Yankee in King Arthur's Court,** *1889.* •1306

Waiting for the German verb is surely the ultimate thrill.

Flann O'Brien, Irish novelist and journalist. •1307

I once heard a Californian student in Heidelberg say, in one of his calmest moods, that he would rather decline two drinks than one German adjective.

Mark Twain, **A Tramp Abroad** *(1880)* •1308

Cast iron rules will not answer... what is one man's colon is another man's comma.

Mark Twain, in **Charles Neider** *(ed.)* **Life as I Find It** *(1961)* •1309

263

I will not go down
to posterity talking
bad grammar.

Benjamin Disreali, while correcting proofs
of his final parliamentary speech; in Robert
Blake, Disreali *(1966)* •1310

This is the sort
of English up
with which I
will not put.

Winston Churchill, in Ernest Gowers,
Plain Words *(1948)* •1311

It is a good thing for an uneducated man to read books of quotations.
Winston Churchill, My Early Life •1314

Next to being witty yourself, the best thing is to quote another's wit.
Christian N. Bovee, American lawyer and author •1312

The nicest thing about quotes is that they give us a nodding acquaintance with the originator which is often socially impressive.
Actor Kenneth Williams, in the preface to Acid Drops, *1980* •1315

A proverb is one man's wit and all men's wisdom.
Lord John Russell, in R.J. Mackintosh, Sir James Mackintosh *(1835)* •1313

265

Do you know, I pick up favourite quotations, and store them in my mind as ready armour, offensive or defensive, amid the struggle of this turbulent existence.
Scottish poet Robert Burns, in a **letter to Mrs Dunlop,** *6 December, 1792* •1316

It would be nice if sometimes the kind things I say were considered worthy of quotation. It isn't difficult, you know, to be witty or amusing when one has something to say that is destructive, but damned hard to be clever and quotable when you are singing someone's praises.

Noël Coward, in **William Marchant, The Pleasure of His Company** *(1981)* •1318

I quote others only the better to express myself.

French essayist Michel do Montaigne, **Essays, Book 1, Chapter 26,** *1580* •1317

I often quote myself — it adds spice to my conversation.

Irish playwright and critic **George Bernard Shaw** •1319

Those who cannot miss an opportunity of saying a good thing… are not to be trusted with the management of any great question.

William Hazlitt,
Characteristics *(1823)* •1320

Pretentious quotations being the surest road to tedium.

H.W. Fowler and F.G. Fowler,
The King's English *(1906)* •1321

If I had a good quote, I'd be wearing it.

American singer and song writer Bob Dylan in reply to a French journalist who asked for 'a good quote', quoted in The Times, *July 1981.*•1322

Misquotation is, in fact, the pride and priviledge of the learned. A widely-read man never quotes accurately, for the rather obvious reason that he has read too widely.

Hesketh Pearson, **Common Misquotations** *(1934)* •1323

What a good thing Adam had. When he said a good thing he knew nobody had said it before.

Mark Twain, **Notebooks** *(1935)* •1324

Oscar Wilde: How I wish I had said that.
Whistler: You will, Oscar, you will.

James McNeill Whistler, in R. Ellman, **Oscar Wilde** *(1987)* •1325

267

Polonius: What do you read, my lord?

Hamlet: Words, words, words.

William Shakespeare, **Hamlet** *(1601)* **II.ii** •1326

No one means all he says, and yet very few say all they mean, for words are slippery and thought is viscous.

Henry Brooks Adams, **The Education of Henry Adams** *(1907)* •1327

'When I use a word,' Humpty Dumpty said in a rather scornful tone, 'it means just what I choose it to mean — neither more nor less.'

Lewis Carroll, **Through the Looking-Glass** *(1872)* •1328

Then you should say what you mean,' the March Hare went on. 'I do,' Alice hastily replied; 'at least - at least I mean what I say — that's the same thing, you know.' 'Not the same thing a bit!' said the Hatter. 'Why, you might just as well say that I see what I eat is the same thing as I eat what I see!'

Lewis Carroll, **Alice's Adventures in Wonderland** *(1865)* •1329

'Contrariwise,' continued Tweedledee, 'if it was so, it might be; and if it were so, it would be: but as it isn't, it ain't. That's logic.

Lewis Carroll,
Through the Looking-Glass
(1872) •1330

The trouble with words is that you never know whose mouths they've been in.

Dennis Potter •1331

The word 'good' has many meanings. For example, if a man were to shoot his grandmother at a range of five hundred yards, I should call him a good shot, but not necessarily a good man.

G.K. Chesterton •1332

I always have a quotation for everything — it saves original thinking.

Detective fiction writer Dorothy L Sayers, in Have His Carcase *(1932)* •1333

Epigram and truth are rarely commensurate. Truth has to be somewhat chiselled, as it were, before it will fit into an epigram.

Joseph Farrell, Lectures of a Certain Professor. •1334

John Wesley's conversation is good, but he is never at leisure. He is always obliged to go at a certain hour. This is very disagreeable to a man who loves to fold his legs and have out his talk, as I do.

Samuel Johnson, in Boswell's Life of Samuel Johnson *(1791) — 25 March 1776* •1335

269

Circumlocution, n. A literary trick whereby the writer who has nothing to say breaks it gently to the reader. *Ambrose Bierce,* The Devil's Dictionary *(1911)* •1336

It was the look which caused her to be known in native bearer and half-caste circles as 'Mogi-Mgumbi', which may be loosely translated as She On Who It Is Unsafe To Try Any Oompus Boompus. *P.G. Wodehouse,* Money in the Bank, *1946* •1337

If nobody ever said anything unless he knew what he was talking about, a ghastly hush would descend upon the earth. *A.P. Herbert, English writer and humorist* •1338

If I reprehend anything in this world, it is the use of my oracular tongue, and a nice derangement of epitaphs! *Richard Brinsley Sheridan,* The Rivals *(1775)* III.iii •1339

He is the very pineapple of politeness!

The Rivals, III.iii •1340

Comparisons are odious.

William Shakespeare, Much Ado About Nothing *(1598-9)* III.v •1342

No caparisons, Miss, if you please! — Caparisons don't become a young woman.

The Rivals, IV.ii •1341

The conclusion of your syllogism, I said lightly, is fallacious, being based upon licenced premises.

Flann O'Brien, At Swim-Two-Birds *(1939)* •1343

True wit is Nature to advantage dressed,

What oft was thought, but ne'er so well expressed.

Alexander Pope, An Essay on Criticism *(1711)* •1344

To become a great writer, whatever you do — avoid piles.

T.S. Eliot •1345

It is always the best policy to speak the truth — unless, of course, you are an exceptionally good liar.

Jerome K. Jerome, in The Idler, *February 1892* •1346

If one tells the truth, one is sure, sooner or later, to be found out.

Oscar Wilde, 'Phrases and Philosophies for the use of the Young', *1894* •1347

Cecil Graham: What is a cynic?

Lord Darlington: A man who knows the price of everything and the value of nothing.

Oscar Wilde, Lady Windermere's Fan, *1892.* •1348

Wit is… the eloquence of indifference.

William Hazlitt, Lectures on English Comic Writers *(1818)* •1349

Never trust a writer who uses his initials.

A.A. Gill •1350

Virginia Woolf subscribed to the theory that the pen was mightier than the sword; and I once saw the mighty Evelyn Waugh reel under a savage blow from her Parker 51.

Alan Bennett, **Forty Years On** *(1969)* •1351

Do not unto others as you would that they should do unto you. Their tastes may not be the same.

George Bernard Shaw, **Man and Superman,** 'Maxims for Revolutionists: The Golden Rule' *(1903)* •1352

I always pass on good advice. It is the only thing to do with it. It is never of any use to oneself.

Oscar Wilde, **An Ideal Husband** *(1895)* •1353

There is only one thing in the world worse than being talked about, and that is not being talked about.

Oscar Wilde, **The Picture of Dorian Gray,** *1891* •1354

If, with the literate, I am impelled to try an epigram, I never asked to take the credit; we all assume that Oscar said it.

Dorothy Parker, 'Oscar Wilde', **Sunset Gun,** *1928* •1355

If you steal from one author, it's plagiarism; if you steal from many it's research.

Wilson Mizner, American playwright •1356

You beat your pate, and fancy wit will come:

Knock as you please, there's nobody at home.

Alexander Pope, 'Epigram: You beat your pate' *(1732)* •1358

When the wine is in, the wit is out.

Thomas Becon, Catechism *(1560)* •1357

How come there's no other name for a thesaurus?

Wright Stevens •1362

Mark my words, when a society has to resort to a lavatory for its humour, the writing is on the wall. *Alan Bennett,* **Forty Years On** *(1969)* •1360

Nominations to find Britain's favourite poem include 'The Rhubarb of O'Mark I am'.

Dennis O'Driscoll •1361

Oh, do let me go on. I want to see how it ends.

Oscar Wilde, having been stopped midway through translating a passage from the Greek version of the New Testament in his viva at Oxford; in James Sutherland (ed.), The Oxford Book of Literary Anecdotes •1359

Index

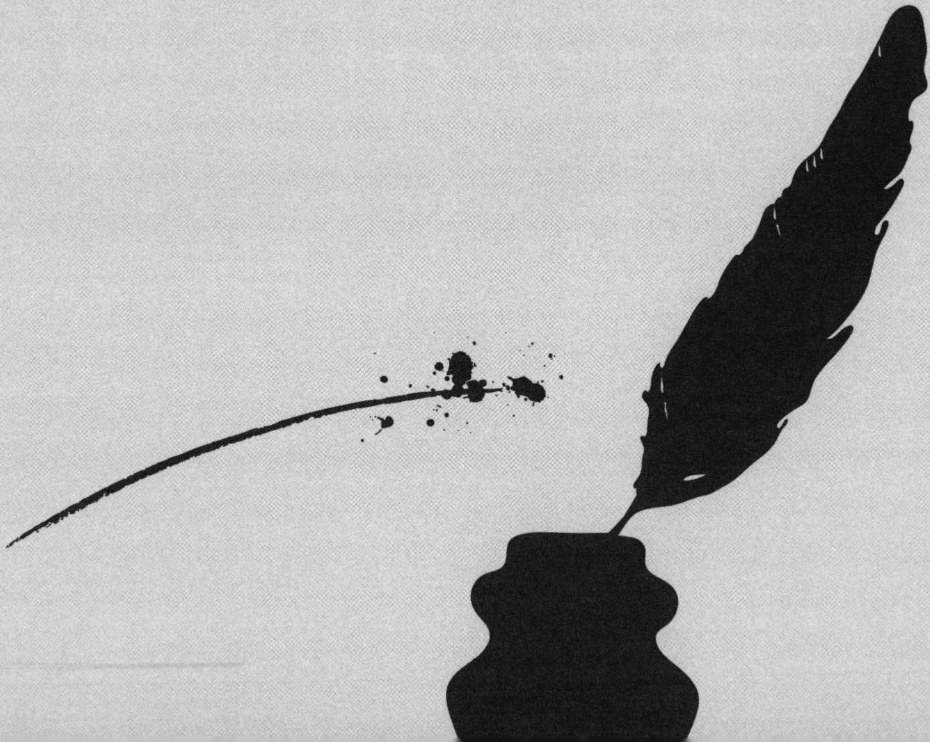

Adams, Douglas •225 *Adams, Henry Brooks* •1327 *Adams, John* •379 *Addison, Joseph* •470, •547, •1102 *Agee, James* •656 *Alcott, Louisa May* •684 *Aldiss, Brian* •512 *Amis, Kingsley* •120, •213, •496, •609, •808 *Andersen, Hans Christian* •1031 *Archer, Jeffrey* •611-613 *Aristotle,* •92, •126, •371, •704, •916, •1147, •1154, •1181 *Arnold, Matthew* •574 *Atwood, Margaret* •28, •82, •110, •211, •269, •1109 *Auden, W.H.* •121, •431, •435, •438, •444, •504, •505, •509, •742, •846, •868, •1011, •1051, •1187 *Augustine, St.* •41, •373, •937 *Austen, Jane* •9, •24, •146, •182, •183, •234-236, •356, •489, •490, •695, •734, •736, •737, •765, •783, •862, •885, •887, •911, •912, •922, •1001, •1004, •1013, •1037, •1075, •1124, •1126-1128, •1130, •1131 *Bacon, Francis* •5, •20, •65, •666, •842, •1012 *Bagehot, Walter* •495, •501 *Balzac, Honoré de* •237, •492, •493, •559, •1052 *Bankhead, Tallulah* •295 *Banks, Iain* •272 *Banks-Smith, Nancy* •526 *Barham, R.H.* •769 *Barnes, Julian* •11, •212, •1062 *Barth, John* •209 *Barthes, Roland* •310 *Bastard, Thomas* •815 *Bawden, Nina* •222 *Beck* •125 *Beckett, Samuel* •142, •210, •515, •606, •957, •992, •999, •1094 *Becon, Thomas* •1357 *Beerbohm, Max* •521, •728 *Behan, Brendan* •261, •453, •1167 *Behn, Aphra* •831, •945 *Bell, Clive* •458, •689 *Bell, Quentin* •689 *Bell, Vanessa* •689 *Belloc, Hilaire* •33, •50, •1138 *Bellow, Saul* •155, •283, •965 *Benchley, Robert* •1078 *Bennett, Alan* •25, •288, •314, •498, •518, •529, •969, •1047, •1155, •1351, •1360 *Bennett, Arnold* •890 *Bentham, Jeremy* •400 *Betjeman, John* •434, •527, •528, •720 *Bible, The* •2, •307, •693, •697, •698, •738, •759, •826, •953, •1033, •1122, •1174 *Bierce, Ambrose* •1161, •1336 *Bishop, Elizabeth* •1115 *Bishop, Jim* •469 *Blake, William* •418, •486, •647, •741, •925 *Book of Common Prayer, The* •780 *Boorstin, Daniel* •1088 *Borges, Jorge Luis* •522 *Boswell, James* •378 *Bovee, Christian N.* •1312 *Bowen, Elizabeth* •775 *Bowles, Paul* •218 *Bradbury, Ray* •114 *Bradstreet, Anne* •416 *Bragg, Melvyn* •1295 *Braque, Georges* •80 *Brecht, Bertolt* •596, •951, •1182 *Breslin, Jimmy* •749 *Bridges, Robert* •1039 *Brodsky, Joseph* •75 *Brontë, Charlotte* •238, •241, •421, •563, •791, •873, •1003, •1060 *Brontë, Emily* •563 *Brookner, Anita* •461 *Brougham, Harry* •561 *Brown, Helen Gurley* •49 *Brown, Rita Mae* •1009 *Browne, Sir Thomas* •1036 *Browning, Elizabeth Barrett,* •187, •756, •855 *Browning, Robert* •809, •870, •1023, •1024 *Buchan, John* •633 *Buchanan, Robert* •921 *Bulwer-Lytton, Edward George* •61, •1183 *Bunyan, John* •105 *Burgess, Anthony* •266, •960, •1132 *Burnett, Frances Hodgson* •1070 *Burney, Fanny* •485, •1005, •1117 *Burns, Robert* •417, •434, •550, •849, •1035, •1316 *Burton, Robert* •232, •415 *Butler, Samuel* •357, •376, •1092, •1268, •1273 *Byatt, A.S.* •39, •300 *Byron, George, Lord* •158, •440, •491, •553-556, •743, •746, •750, •755, •897, •943, •944, •968, •1026, •1136 *Calvino, Italo* •320 *Campbell, Roy* •523 *Camus, Albert* •1010, •1997 *Carey, John* •473, •484, •513, •520, •528, •529 *Carey, Peter* •277, •1282, •1283, •1289 *Carlyle, Thomas* •284, •562 *Carpenter, Humphrey* •286, •298 *Carroll, Lewis* •57, •157, •349, •451, •500, •572, •714, •1042, •1266, •1299, •1328-1330 *Carter, Angela* •42, •336, •360 *Cather, Willa* •49 *Cato the Elder* •150 *Cecil, Lord David* •58, •497 *Cerf, Bennett* •530 *Cervantes, Miguel de* •113 *Chandler, Raymond* •86, •202, •347, •397, •872, •915, •1113, •1300 *Channon, Henry 'Chips'* •7, •296 *Chateaubriand, François-René* •130 *Chatterton, Thomas* •530 *Chaucer, Geoffrey* •844, •847, •889, •917, •918, •939, *Chekhov, Anton* •143, •245, •506, •891, •980, •1193 *Chesterfield, Lord* •18 *Chesterton,G.K.* •171, •321, •513, •1164, •1332 *Chomsky, Noam* •1297 *Christie, Agatha* •414, •526 *Churchill, Winston* •1311, •1314 *Cicero* •37, •800, •1148, •1159, *Clark, Mary Higgins* •462 *Clarke, Creston* •535 *Clough, Arthur Hugh* •829 *Coleridge, Samuel Taylor* •72, •387, •487, •488, •530, •552, •688 *Colman, George (The Elder)* •913 *Compton-Burnett, Ivy* •995 *Confucius* •718 *Congreve, William* •754 *Connolly, Cyril* •136, •259, •315, •447, •599 *Conrad, Joseph* •46, •246, •510, •583, •584, •752 *Cope, Wendy* •410, •445 *Coren, Alan* •949 *Cotterell, Geoffrey* •1093 *Courteline, Georges* •725 *Coward, Noël* •154, •785, •805, •1318 *Cowper, William* •293 *Creasey, John* •1111 *Crisp, Quentin* •206, •299, •727 *Cummings, e.e.* •928 *Dante Alighieri* •532, •757, •983 *Darrow, Clarence* •1068 *Darwin, Charles* •145 *Davies, Andrew* •737 *Davies, John* •861 *Davies, Robertson* •19, •43, •68, •168, •350 *Davies, W.H.* •700, •975 *Dawson, George* •14 *Debray, Régis* •493 *Dench, Judi* •368 *Denham, John* •997 *Descartes, René* •48 *Dickens, Charles* •494-498, •516, •567, •652, •706, •708, •768, •784, •881, •886, •898, •1018, •1134, •1145, •1152, •1153, •1267 *Diderot, Denis* •44 *Didion, Joan* •228 *Dillon, Wentworth* •51 *Disraeli, Benjamin* •239, •242, •865, •875, •1310 *Doctorow, E.L.* •217, •323 *Donaldson, Stephen* •343 *Donne, John* •807, •905, •927, •990, •993 *Douglas, O.* •197

Dowson, Ernest •790 Doyle, Sir Arthur Conan •333, •339, •970 Dryden, John •149, •778, •850, •851 Dumas, Alexandre ('Dumas père') •1072 Dumas, Alexandre (Fils) •672 Dylan, Bob •1322 Eco, Umberto •34, •89, •122 Eddington, Sir Arthur •27 Edelman, Maurice •1192 Einstein, Albert •499 Eliot, George •188, •573, •882, •1141, •1288 Eliot, T.S. •87, •393, •428, •429, •438, •787, •797, •799, •955, •986, •1345 Elizabeth I (Queen of England) •305 Ellis, Alice Thomas •681 Emerson, Ralph Waldo •63, •185, •711, •713, •1123 Empson, William •433 Etheridge, Sir George •179 Eyre, Richard •483 Farquhar, George •370 Farrell, Joseph •1334 Faulkner, William •109 Ferber, Edna •1050 Fielding, Helen •275 Fielding, Henry •722, •941, •942 Fields, W.C •961 Fitzgerald, F. Scott •90, •129, •174, •516,. 972, •1303 Flaubert, Gustave •101, •118, •240, •388, •468, •480, •1057 Fletcher, Phineas •947 Foot, Michael •1157 Ford, Ford Madox •175 Ford, John •877 Ford, Richard •108 Forster, E.M. •13, •16, •71, •117, •159, •260, •586 Fowler, F.G. •1321 Fowler, H.W. •1321 Frank, Anne •1046 Franklin, Benjamin •758, •789 Franzen, Jonathan •52, •1103 Freud, Sigmund •292, •597 Frost, Robert •395, •835 Fuller, Thomas •895, •1125 Galbraith, J.K. •107 Gallant, Mavis •215 Galsworthy, John •1285 Gardner, John •156 Garrick, David •913 Gautier, Theophile •854 Gay, John •948 George III (King of Great Britain & Ireland) •478 Gibran, Kahlil •858, •893 Gibson, William •348 Gide, André •166, •915, •524 Gilbert, Sandra M. •1000 Gill, A.A. •1350 Giraudoux, Jean •394 Gladstone, W.E. •531 Goethe, Johann Wolfgang von •479, •803, •894 Goldberg, Natalie •216 Golden, Harry •1158 Goldsmith, Oliver •730, •810 Goldwyn, Sam •481 Gordon, Mary •219 Grahame, Kenneth •585 Grant, Duncan •689 Graves, Robert •482 Gray, Thomas •382, •549, •717 Grayson, Helen •160 Greene, Graham •119, •162, •173, •675, •1083, •1110 Greer, Germaine •413 Gregory the Great •1017 Gunn, Thom •411 Hampton, Christopher •475 Hand, Leonard •1274 Harding, Warren G. •588 Hardy, Thomas •152, •883, •950 Harris, Joel Chandler •814 Hartley, L.P. •338, •985 Hawthorne, Nathaniel •880 Haycox, Ernest •1056 Hazlitt, William •487, •488, •1007, •1320, •1349 Heaney, Seamus •412, •438, •1053 Heilbrun, Carolyn G. •456 Heine, Heinrich •1095, •1188 Heinemann, William •1112 Heller, Joseph •273 Hellman, Lillian •227 Helvetius •1189 Hemingway, Ernest •138, •257, •450, •503, •516, •600, •860, •929

Herbert, A.P. •1151, •1338 Herrick, Robert •801, •876 Hiaasen, Carl •115 Hitchcock, Alfred •99 Hobbes, Thomas •794, •1160 Holmes, Oliver Wendell •804, •1265 Holub, Miroslav •412 Homer •531, •540, •748 Hope, Anthony •1137 Horace •116, •372, •744, •1120, •1165, •1272 Housman, A.E. •745, •819 Howells, William Dean •176 Hughes, Shirley •88, •330 Hughes, Ted •438, •440, •1283 Hughes, Thomas •710 Hugo, Victor •1045 Humphries, Barry •466 Huxley, Aldous •594, •772, •923, •1058 Ibsen, Henrik •365 Innes, Hammond •30 Ishiguro, Kazuo •169 Jakobson, Roman •427 James I (James VI of Scotland) •304 James, Brian •1116 James, Henry •79, •93, •141, •164, •243, •249, •511, •576-578, •735, •1030, •1087 James, P.D. •332 Jameson, Henry •502 Jay, Antony •1142 Jerome, Jerome K. •747, •1346 Johnson, Samuel (from Boswell's Life of Samuel Johnson) •60, •181, •285, •378, •380, •463, •705, •719, •732, •974, •1064, •1140, •1176, •1335 Johnson, Samuel •8, •47, •97, •180, •448, •485, , •788, •837, •892, •1072, •1281 Jong, Erica •53 Jonson, Ben •476, •543, •836 Joyce, James •514, •515, •589, •589, •1271 Julian of Norwich •991 Juvenal •691, •978 Kafka, Franz •62, •518, •964 Kaufman, George S. •1063 Keats, John •384, •385, •866, •907, •971 Kerouac, Jack •607 Kilpatrick, James J. •170 King, Stephen, •337 Kingsolver, Barbara •932 Kipling, Rudyard •508, •509, •687, •920, •1262 Knox, James •434 Koran, The •1 Kraus, Karl •1163 Kundera, Milan •140, •287 Kyd, Thomas •982 Lacan, Jacques •1277 Lahr, John •467 Lamb, Charles •552, •820 Langland, William •1296 Lardner, Ring •1114 Larkin, Philip •69, •401, •408, •436-438, •527, •699, •924 Lawrence, D.H. •26, •354, •359, •571, •591-593, Le Guin, Ursula •214, •340 Lear, Edward •504 Lebowitz, Fran •22, •70, •1081 Lehmann, Rosamund •608 Leonard, Elmore •172 Lessing, Doris •12, •221 Lette, Kathy •679 Levin, Bernard •1305 Lewis, C.S. •342, •525, •760 Lichtenberg, Georg C. •21, •477 Liebling, A.J. •1190 Lincoln, Abraham •449, •1179 Lodge, David •204 Longfellow, Henry Wadsworth •564, •664 Lurie, Alison •329 Luther, Martin •29 Lydgate, John •968 Lynch, David •115 Macaulay, Lord •153, •560, •1172 MacGowan, Shane •103 Machiavelli, Niccolò •1156 MacLeish, Archibald •392 MacNeice, Louis •439 MacNeil, Robert •1264 Madonna •59 Malouf, David •457 Mansfield, Katherine •252, •506, •517, •587, •1043 Marlowe, Christopher •530, •771 Marquis, Don •165, •396 Martial •230, •770, •977, •1090

Marvell, Andrew •795 Marx, Groucho •406 Marx, Karl •493
Masefield, John •648 Maugham, W. Somerset •402, •446,
•683, •774, •813, •904, •933, •1084 McBain, Ed •334 McCarthy,
Justin •763 McEwan, Ian •220, •226 McLeod, Fiona •909
Melville, Herman •565 Meredith, George •1034 Meredith,
Owen •190 Merrill, James •1294 Millay, Edna St. Vincent
•661 Miller, Arthur •148, •1185, •1263 Miller, Henry •318, •363,
•1104 Miller, J. Hillis •522 Milne, A.A. •596, •685, •973, •1304
Milton, John •131, •377, •433, •522, •545, •674, •745, •874
Mitchell, Adrian •405 Mitford, Nancy •602, •603 Mizner,
Wilson •1356 Molière (Jean-Baptiste Poquelin) •1284
Montaigne •231, •669, •1317 Moore, Brian •55 Moore,
Marianne •1302 Moore, Thomas •899 Morell, Thomas •1175
Morris, William •575 Morris, Wright •167 Morrison, Toni
•268, •1106 Mortimer, John •316, •963, •1194 Mosley, Walter
•95 Motion, Andrew •443 Muggeridge, Malcolm •353
Murdoch, Iris •1029 Murray, John Middleton •587 Nabokov,
Vladimir •147, •940, •1061 Naipaul, V.S. •267, •276 Nash,
Ogden •657, •677, •793, •822 Nichols, Peter •265, •471
Nicolson, Harold •507 Nin, Anais •203 O'Brien, Flann •686,
•1307, •1343 O'Connor, Flannery •207, •673, •1098 O'Connor,
Frank •O'Driscoll, Dennis •1361 O'Rourke, P.J. •346
Orton, Joe •73 Orwell, George •139, •601, •1008, •1014, •1091,
•1100, •1144 Ovid •319, •900, •1129 Owen, Wilfred •426, •166,
•1170, •1186 Paget, Francis E. •189 Parker, Dorothy •653, •914,
•1355 Pascal, Blaise •77, •841, •1270 Passos, John Dos •934
Pasternak, Boris •996 Peacock, Thomas Love •959 Pearson,
Hesketh •1323 Pepys, Samuel •546, •781 Peter, Laurence J.
•1191 PetievichvGerald •91 Philips, Ambrose •777 Pinker,
Steven •1261 Plath, Sylvia •440, •655, •680 Plato •667, •701,
•703, •903, •908, •1146 Pliny the Younger •151 Poe, Edgar
Allan •530 Pope, Alexander •85, •177, •484, •530, •659, •817,
•821, •994, •998, •1016, •1121, •1139, •1269, •1344, •1358 Potter,
Dennis •290, •1331 Pound, Ezra •311, •762 Powell, Anthony
•32 Pratchett, Terry •35, •345, •935, •1074 Priestley, J.B. •782
Pritchett, V.S. •327 Proust, Marcel •516 Quasimodo,
Salvatore •404 Quennell, Peter •524 Raleigh, Walter •358,
•823 Rankin, Ian •278 Rascoe, Burton •200 Rawson, Clayton
•1069 Reed, Lou •409 Renard, Jules •1065 Rendell, Ruth •274
Reyner, Edward •1279 Rhys, Jean •264, •1015 Rice, Grantland
•830 Richardson, Samuel •548 Roberts, Michèle •1059
Rochefoucauld, Duc de la •906 Rochester, Earl of (John

Wilmot) •845 Rodin, Auguste •492 Roosevelt, Franklin D.
•1184 Rossetti, Christina •244, •690, •984 Rossetti, Dante
Gabriel •690 Rousseau, Jean-Jacques •31, •233 Rowling, J.K.
•279, •280, •1118 Rushdie, Salman •76, •78, •100, •133, •1195
Ruskin, John •17, •303, •1032 Russell, Bertrand •15, •66, •308
Russell, Lord John •1313 Saki •723, •1133 Salinger, J.D. •651,
•919 Sandburg, Carl •390, •1286 Santayana, George •104
Sapper (Herman Cyril McNeile) •633 Saro-Wiwa, Ken
•1198, •1200 Sartre, Jean-Paul •605, •967 Sassoon, Siegfried
•1169 Saussure, Ferdinand de •1278 Sayers, Dorothy L. •1333
Sayre, Murray •639 Schiller, Friedrich von •98 Scott, Paul
•966 Scott, Sir Walter •341, •489, •490, •540, •558, •1038, •1066
Searle, Ronald •399, •716 Sellar, W.C. •712 Shakespeare,
William •4, •178, •210, •368, •375, •476-483, •522, •533-543, •646,
•663, •671, •692, •694, •724, •726, •753, •779, •792, •806, •811, •812,
•825, •827, •833, •834, •838, •840, •848, •848, •852, •856, •859, •864,
•884, •888, •896, •901, •902, •936, •938, •976, •981, •1025, •1135,
•1150, •1173, •1252, •1326, •1342 Shaw, George Bernard •247,
•507, •582, •1096, •1101, •1177, •1287, •1318, •1352 Shelley, Mary
•557 Shelley, Percy Bysshe •386, •419, •491, •1280 Sheridan,
Richard Brinsley •454, •1339-1341 Shields, Carol •40, •223
Sidney, Sir Philip •106, •374, •853, •952 Simenon, Georges
•1049 Singer, Isaac Bashevis •229 Sitwell, Edith •403, •590
Smiles, Samuel •733 Smith, Dodie •979 Smith, Logan
Pearsall •56, •665, •1089 Smith, Stevie •124 Smith, Sydney
•420, •474, Smith, Zadie •45, •281 Sontag, Susan •224
Sophocles •863, •903, •952 Southey, Robert •1060 Spark,
Muriel •208, •263, •271, •442 Spencer, Herbert •731 Spender,
Stephen •598, •1168 Spenser, Edmund •3, •522, •1290 Squire,
J.C. •1071 Stassinopoulos, Ariana •614 Steele, Richard •64
Stein, Gertrude •464 Steinbeck, John •23 Steiner, George
•132 Stendhal (Henri Beyle) •135, •184 Sterne, Laurence
•649, •857 Stevens, Wallace •398 Stevens, Wright •1362
Stevenson, Adlai •1097 Stevenson, Robert Louis •10, •67,
•134, •192, •322, •328, •668, •670, •1054 Stoppard, Tom •317,
•361, •362, •367, •514, •1076, •1162 Stowe, Harriet Beecher •650
Strunk, William •196 Styron, William •54 Swift, Graham
•81, •459 Swift, Jonathan •137, •352, •824, •1020 Tacitus •1086,
•1149 Taylor, Ann •682 Taylor, D.J. •1072 Taylor, Jane •682
Tennyson, Alfred, Lord •421, •431, •568, •569, •832, •867, •1079
Terence •102 Terry, Ellen •500 Thackeray, William
Makepeace •501 Thiong'o, Ngugi wa •1196

Thomas, Dylan •258, •414, •430, •432, •441, •486, •798, •869, •956 *Thoreau, Henry David* •111, •566 *Thucydides* •1199 *Thurber, James* •1107 *Tibbon, Judah Ibn* •36 *Tolkein, J.R.R.* •344, •345, •351, •1298 *Tolstoy, Leo* •83, •186, •499, •766 *Tomalin, Nicholas,* •1178 *Townsend, Sue* •294 *Trevor, William* •326 *Trillin, Calvin* •1105 *Trollope, Anthony* •161, •325, •502, •721, •910, •926, •1055 *Trollope, Frances 'Fanny'* •123 *Turgenev, Ivan* •1041, *Twain, Mark* •74, •191, •194, •198, •248, •250, •312, •313, •389, •503, •508, •579, •678, •767, •773, •878, •879, •987, •1006, •1019, •1022, •1073, •1077, •1291, •1306, •1308, •1309, •1324 *Tyler, Anne* •282 *Tynan, Kenneth* •366, •465, •472, •516, •525 *Updike, John,* •364, •1080 *Victoria, Queen* •494, •619 *Vidal, Gore* •210 *Virgil* •871 *Voltaire* •1085, •1171, •1189, •1249 *Wain, John* •407 *Walker, Alice* •1040 *Wallace, Irving* •452 *Wallace, William Ross* •676 *Walpole, Horace* •958 *Warhol, Andy* •930 *Waugh, Evelyn* •94, •163, •205, •256, •302, •516, •707, •1143 *Webster, John* •544, •802, *Weldon, Fay* •931, •1067 *Wellington, Duke of (Arthur Wellesley)* •1119 *Wells, H.G.* •112, •255, •510-512 *Wesker, Arnold* •702 *West, Rebecca* •254 *Wharton, Edith* •176, •251 *Whately, Richard* •306 *Whistler, James McNeill* •1325 *White, Patrick* •96, •270 *Whitman, Walt* •422, •570, •571, •1027, •1028, •1180 *Wilde, Oscar* •6, •128, •144, •193, •289, •291, •297, •331, •369, •423, •424, •505, •567, •580, •709, •729, •740, •751, •776, •989, •1002, •1021, •1347, •1348, •1353, •1354, •1359 *Willans, Geoffrey* •399, •716 *Williams, Kenneth* •1315 *Williams, Tennessee* •210, •786, •1048 *Wilson, Angus* •1301 *Winterson, Jeanette* •84, •301, •355 *Wittgenstein, Ludwig* •1276 *Wodehouse, P.G.* •199, •764, •1082, •1099, •1337 *Wolfe, Thomas* •253 *Wollstonecraft, Mary* •696 *Woolf, Virginia* •201, •309, •324, •335, •455, •460, •517, •519, •521, •522, •547, •595, •1275, •1292 *Wordsworth, William* •381, •383, •410, •423, •551, •654, •658, •660, •662, •828, •1044 *Wycherley, William* •946 *Yates, Dornford (Cecil William Mercer)* •633 *Yeatman, R.J.* •712 *Yeats, W.B.* •391, •425, •519, •520, •816, •818, •954 *Young, Edward* •761, •796 *Zweig, Arnold* •2922